GRILLING

GRILLING

Eric Treuillé & Birgit Erath

Photography by
IAN O'LEARY

LONDON, NEW YORK, MUNICH
MELBOURNE, DELHI

EDITORIAL CONSULTANT
Rosie Kindersley
DESIGN AND ART DIRECTION
Stuart Jackman
PROJECT EDITOR
Julia Pemberton Hellums
EDITOR
Sally Somers
US EDITOR
Barbara Berger
US RECIPE CONSULTANTS
Wesley Martin, Barbara Bowman
PRODUCTION CONTROLLER
Elizabeth Cherry

FOOD STYLING
Eric Treuillé

DEDICATION
To our families, in London,
Germany, and France, in fond
memory of much outdoor feasting.

First paperback edition published
in the United States in 2007 by
DK Publishing
375 Hudson Street
New York, NY 10014

07 08 09 10 10 9 8 7 6 5 4 3 2 1

A catalog record for this book is available from
the Library of Congress
ISBN 9-780-7566-1887-2

Color reproduction in Italy by GRB

Printed and bound by
L. Rex Printing Company Ltd, China

Discover more at
www.dk.com

CONTENTS

INTRODUCTION

All around the world people cook over open fire. It's how cooking began and it has stood the test of time. It's today's favorite way to cook and it is easy to understand why. Grilling means no fuss, less fat, more flavor, most fun. Nothing brings out the best flavor in food quite like eating it sizzling hot off the grill.

Good food means a good time, and a gathering around the grill makes any meal a celebration. Friends and family mix, mingle, and unwind as steaks sear and ribs sizzle. Casual, yet a real occasion, a barbecue sets appetites on fire.

There's something elemental about open-fire cooking. Could it be that those dancing flames, glowing embers, and smoky aromas awaken our long-lost primordial selves?

Even people with the most hard-boiled "I can't cook" attitudes are unable to resist the excitement of cooking over hot coals. We don't want to get too serious, because, to us, grilling isn't serious. This book is not a heavy-weight volume crammed with everything you need to know to grill like a pro. It's about having fun outdoors with food, flavor, and fire.

Grilling shouldn't mean burnt steak, scorched chicken, and other charred remains. Say goodbye to all that. Say hello to great grilled food every time. We've identified the key factors to guarantee grilling success, and we've made them simple.

To make our recipes, all you need are a few ingredients, hot coals and a sense of adventure. So relax. Just do it. Because we all love food hot off the grill. Come outside and join the party!

Eric Begus

NOTES FROM THE COOKS

BEFORE YOU COOK read through the recipe carefully. Make sure you have all the equipment and ingredients required. In all recipes, vegetables are washed and peeled, unless otherwise stated.

ON PREHEATING

We have given instructions for indoor broiling as well as outdoor grilling. But, whether cooking outdoors or indoors, be sure to allow enough time to get your grill or broiler up to the desired firepower. Successful grilling must sear the surface of food quickly to form a flavorful crust and to seal the succulent juices inside. Inadequate preheating means the crust does not form, the juices leak out, and you have uniformly tough, dry, and tasteless results.

For charcoal grills, light up 30–40 minutes before you want to start grilling. This gives the coals time to reach the perfect temperature for a hot fire.

For gas grills, allow 10–15 minutes to preheat the lava rocks to the desired temperature.

For ridged cast-iron grill pans, set over a medium-high heat 3 minutes before grilling. To see if it is hot enough, splash a few drops of water on the surface: they should sizzle and evaporate immediately.

For broilers, allow 5–10 minutes to preheat an electric broiler and 3–5 minutes for a gas broiler before you want to start.

ON TASTING

Always taste food as you cook and before you serve. Don't be afraid to add or change flavors to suit your palate—what's fun about cooking is experimenting, improvising, creating. Ingredients differ from day to day, season to season and kitchen to kitchen. Be prepared to the adjust sweetness, sharpness, spiciness, and, most important of all, salt to your own taste. The amount of salt and pepper used to season food makes the difference between good and great food.

SALT AND PEPPER

As a general guideline, allow 2 tsp salt and 1 tsp pepper for every 4 servings of meat. In practice, ingredients vary, palates vary, and even salts vary, but this remains a good guideline.

ON MEASURING

Accurate measurements are essential if you want the same good results each time you follow a recipe.

A good set of measuring cups is the most accurate way to measure dry ingredients.

We recommend using cooks' measuring spoons when following a recipe. All spoon measurements in the book are level unless otherwise stated. To measure dry ingredients with a spoon, scoop the ingredient lightly from the storage container, then level the surface with the edge of a straight-bladed knife.

We use standard level spoon measurements:
    1 tablespoon= ½ fluid ounce
    1 teaspoon= ⅙ fluid ounce

To measure liquids, choose a transparent glass or plastic measuring cup. Always place the cup on a flat surface and check for accuracy at eye level when pouring in a liquid to measure.

A final and important rule of measuring—never measure ingredients over the mixing bowl!

THE GRILL

THE BASIC EQUIPMENT
A grill is a grill is a grill. All you need is a fire, some food and a rack so that the food doesn't actually end up in the fire. That's it. Anything from the latest, state-of-the-art model of barbecue grill to a simple set-up of a rack over a few stones on the beach will pretty much do the same job.

THE RULES FOR SAFETY AND SUCCESS
Get ahead. Our recipes are designed to let you know what steps can be done in advance. Follow our THINK AHEAD instructions, so that when it's time to get grilling, you're all set.

Get organized. Be sure to have everything you need on hand. Outdoor grilling is high-speed, high-heat cooking. Once the food hits the flames, there's no time to run back to the kitchen for tongs, salt, or platter.

Let it be. Food will always stick to the grill rack initially, but once a crisp crust has formed, it can be turned or moved with ease. Don't poke, prod, or attempt to turn food during the first minute of cooking.

Don't crowd the grill. An overloaded grill means food will steam, not sear. You don't want to miss out on the crisply caramelized crust that makes great grilled food what it is.

Check frequently for doneness. Use our suggested cooking times as a guideline. Start checking a few minutes before the food is due to be done. Once food is overcooked, it is tough and dry, and there's no turning the clock back.

Don't wander off. On the safety front, you are, after all, playing with fire, and accidents can happen. On the culinary front, food cooks quickly over hot coals and deserting your post can mean the difference between chargrilled and downright charred.

Clean up. A clean grill rack stops food from sticking. A grill rack encrusted with burnt food results in coals that flare up and new food that tastes of old food. Brush the grill rack with a stiff wire brush while it is still hot, to loosen any charred remains.

THE TOOLS

There are only a few accessories that we feel are really essential for grilling, with good-quality, long-handled tongs and a long metal spatula at the top of the list.

1 Long-handled tongs

2 Long metal spatula

3 Hinged grill rack (round or square)

4 Flat metal skewers

5 Natural bristle basting brush

6 Bamboo skewers

7 Instant-read thermometer

8 Stiff wire brush for cleaning grill

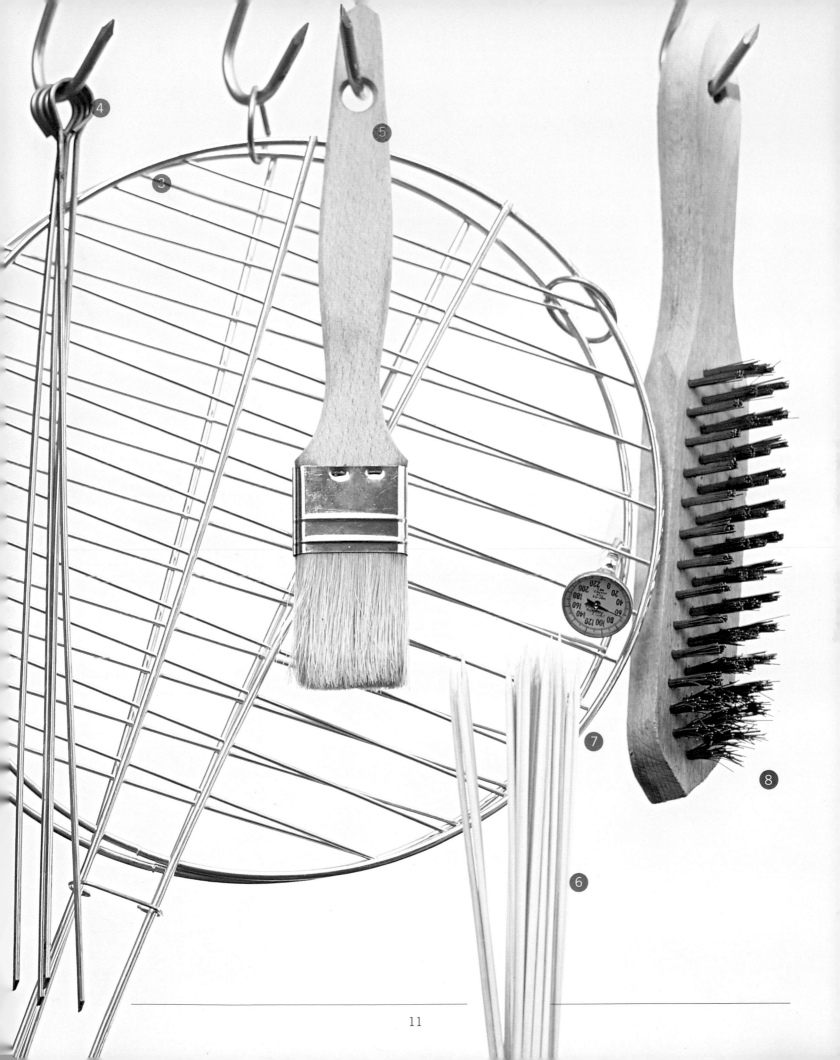

THE FIRE

Heat control is key to successful grilling over charcoal. Building a good fire and judging its temperature are more crucial to success than the type or brand of barbecue grill you own or which type of fuel you use.

HOW TO BUILD IT

How much charcoal you use depends on how much and what kind of food you intend to grill. The more food you are cooking, the longer your fire needs to burn hot.

Keep in mind that it's easier to reduce heat than to raise it, so, as a general rule, start out with more charcoal than you think you'll need.

Spread the charcoal in an even layer about 2 inches deep and 2 inches wider on all sides than the total surface area of the food you are going to grill.

HOW HOT?

The appropriate time to test the temperature of a fire is when the flames have died down. The coals should be glowing red and covered with a light dusting of fine gray ash.

For an approximate guide, hold the palm of your hand flat about 5 inches above the coals and count in seconds.

If you can only keep your hand there for:
- 1–2 seconds - the coals are hot
- 3–4 seconds - the coals are medium hot
- 5–6 seconds - the coals are medium
- 6–7 seconds - the coals are medium low
- 8–9 seconds - the coals are low

HOW TO CONTROL IT

If the fire burns too hot, reduce the heat by spreading out the coals.

If the fire burns too low, boost the heat by pushing the coals closer together and adding more charcoal to the outer edges of the fire.

For a two-level fire with hotter and cooler areas, spread some of the hot coals out in a single layer, to create an area of slightly lower heat to one side of the barbecue. Use the hand test (see above) to check the difference in heat intensity. You can then grill ingredients requiring different cooking temperatures simultaneously.

THE FOOD - DONENESS

Exact grilling times are difficult to predict. Fires burn differently under different conditions. Various factors out of your control, including wind and temperature, make outdoor cooking an empirical, rather than an exact, science. Use our suggested cooking times as a guideline. Watch the clock and check food a few minutes before it is due to be done. Never wait until food is on the plate; always check at the grill.

Experienced chefs and seasoned grill-meisters rely on the touch test (see below) for dense meat like beef, lamb, and pork. We think it is also important to double-check for doneness with a knife. When grilling more delicate things like fish and chicken, use the methods illustrated below. For grilled chicken on the bone, because of the health issues, we urge a policy of seeing is believing.

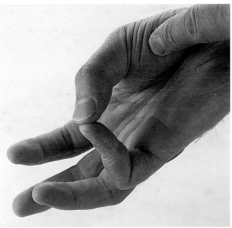

FORK TEST FOR FISH
Use a fork to prod the fish gently. It is done when the flesh is firm, just beginning to flake and opaque through the center but still moist.

KNIFE TEST FOR CHICKEN
Make a cut into the meat with a small, sharp knife. The flesh should be opaque throughout with no trace of pink at the bone.

TOUCH TEST FOR MEAT
The basic principle of the touch test is that meats become firmer as heat penetrates from the surface to the center. Press the thickest part of the meat with your fingertip. The softer the meat is, the rarer it is. The firmer it is, the more well-done it is. The touch test is a skill that can take some practice, but there is an easy shortcut for novice cooks. Press the meat with your finger. Compare the feel of the meat with the feel of the base of your thumb, as you move your thumb from fingertip to fingertip. The thumb muscle tenses and becomes progressively more resistant, corresponding to the different stages of doneness.

For rare, have your thumb touching your index finger (see above, top left).
For medium rare, have your thumb touching your middle finger (see above, top right).
For medium, have your thumb touching your ring finger (see above, bottom left).
For well done, have your thumb touching your pinkie finger (see above, bottom right).

13

FLAVORS FOR THE GRILL

THE KNOWLEDGE

THE PRINCIPLES

From a simple drizzle of olive oil to a complex blend of aromatic spices, there's a world of different flavors to transform grilled food into a bigger and bolder taste experience. There are two main ways of flavoring grilled food: before food is grilled and after food is removed from the fire.

• Flavoring before grilling generally calls for immersing food in a marinade or flavor mix. This immersion can be as brief as a quick dip or as lengthy as an overnight soak.

• Flavoring after grilling focuses on adding an extra flavor dimension to food hot off the grill. Sauces and salsas (pages 130–143) can be served as a flavorful complement to just-grilled foods. Spice mixes (pages 22–25) can be sprinkled or drizzled over food hot off the grill.

• Marinades and flavor mixes are composed of three key elements: acids, oils, and flavorings. These elements perform three distinct functions: to tenderize, moisten, and flavor.

ACIDS: TENDERIZE AND ADD FLAVOR

Citrus juices, vinegars, and yogurt are all acid ingredients that will boost the intensity of any marinade with a bright, sharp tang. Here are a few general tips:

• Use freshly squeezed citrus juices for maximum zing.

• Choose your vinegar according to the level of acid bite you want in your marinade.

• Balsamic vinegar is the most versatile of vinegars. A combination of sweet and sharp, it is ideal for a marinade or to drizzle lightly over food hot from the fire.

• Yogurt is a uniquely all-purpose acid for marinating. It moistens as well as flavors and tenderizes.

OILS: PROVIDE MOISTURE

Lean, tender foods, such as fish and chicken, require the added moisture and protection provided by oil to combat the fierce heat of the fire. More resilient ingredients, such as beef and lamb, when marinated in acidic mixes, require oil to replace the moisture drawn out of the meat by the acid.

• Light, neutral oils, such as canola, contribute little flavor, but there are many other oils that have their own distinctive taste. Try using extra virgin olive oil or a nutty toasted sesame oil (see pages 20–21) for additional flavor.

• Oils can play their moisture-giving role at any stage of the grilling process: in marinades, as a baste during grilling, and as a flavor-packed mix to drizzle over grilled food just before serving.

ADDED FLAVORS

Sweet flavorings take the sharp edge off an acidic marinade. Adding a bit of sugar to a flavor mix enhances the grilling process by helping to create a crispy caramelized crust on food exposed to the fire. Choose sweet flavorings that also add an extra dimension of flavor. We count fragrant honey, dark brown sugar, and tangy pomegranate molasses (see pages 20 & 159) among our favorites.

Fresh flavorings add a fresh fragrance and depth to flavor mixes. Onions and garlic are pungent and vibrant. Asian flavors such as fresh ginger and lemon grass contribute a bright zing (see pages 20–21).

Fresh herbs should be chosen with care for the grill. Woody, robust herbs, such as oregano, rosemary, and thyme, stand up to the strong flavor of food roasted over an open fire. Prolonged cooking over fierce heat eliminates the fragrant perfume of delicate herbs. Reserve them for making stuffings and for quickly grilled foods only.

Dried herbs are ideal flavor mixes for the grill (see pages 20–21). They contain aromatic oils that burst back into life when combined with the moisture of oil and the heat of the fire. Renew your supply of dried herbs regularly. On the grill, stale dried herbs will taste burnt and musty.

SALT AND PEPPER

Salt and pepper are extremely important flavorings for all grilled foods. Salt, however, draws out moisture, and with the moisture flavor, from uncooked food, so always add salt after grilling. For maximum flavor, pepper should be freshly ground or cracked (see page 19). A good pepper grinder is an essential item for all cooks who value real flavor.

• Our preference is always for sea salt, fine or flaked (see page 19).

• Soy sauce (both Chinese and Japanese), fish sauce, and miso are the salts of Asia (see pages 19 & 159). When using, you should not require additional salt.

CHILES

Don't be afraid of chiles—the capsicum family offers much more than just the addition of fiery heat. With so many different varieties available in so many different forms, barbecue cooks have a fabulous range of flavors at their fingertips.

• Look out for "pure" chili powders ground from one variety of chile (see page 18). No kitchen cupboard is complete without red pepper flakes, Tabasco, and Thai sweet chili sauce (see pages 19 & 158).

THE SPICE
SALT, PEPPER, & CHILES

Discerning use of seasoning makes the difference between good and great food. Professional chefs constantly taste their food for levels of salt and heat. The quality of salt matters, as different salts have different flavors and different levels of saltiness. We prefer sea salt, fine or flaked.

Nothing compares with the flavor of freshly ground pepper. A pepper grinder is an essential kitchen tool for any cook. Chiles come in many varieties and forms. Whether fresh, dry, or bottled, chiles will contribute flavor and aroma as well as peppery heat.

1 Crushed red pepper flakes

2 Ancho chili powder

3 Kashmiri chili powder

4 Scotch bonnets

5 Fresh red and green chiles

6 Chipotle peppers in adobo

7 Chinese hot chili sauce

8 Thai sweet chili sauce

9 Tabasco sauce

10 Thai fish sauce

11 Soy sauce

12 Coarse sea salt

13 Fine sea salt

14 Peppercorns

15 Freshly ground pepper

THE SPICE
ADDED FLAVORS

Dedicated grill chefs should boast an international array
of flavorings, condiments, and sauces in their kitchen cupboard.
Here are a few of our favorite flavorings from the global pantry.

1 Herbes de Provence
2 Greek oregano
3 Mexican oregano
4 Pomegranate molasses
5 Toasted sesame oil
6 Hoisin sauce
7 Rice wine vinegar
8 Citrus fruits
9 Red wine vinegar
10 Balsamic vinegar
11 Olive oil
12 Onions
13 Garlic
14 Smoked paprika
15 Hungarian paprika
16 Annatto
17 Tamarind
18 Miso
19 Wasabi
20 Fresh ginger

21 Pickled ginger
22 Lemon grass

21

CAROLINA HONEY GLAZE

MAKES ½ CUP
2 tsp cajun seasoning
2 tbsp Dijon mustard
¼ cup honey
2 tbsp cider vinegar or orange juice

Combine seasoning, mustard, honey, and vinegar or juice. Use to marinate pork ribs up to 1 day in advance of grilling, pork chops up to 4 hours in advance, chicken wings up to 8 hours in advance, and chicken breasts up to 4 hours in advance. Brush on more during grilling.

THINK AHEAD
Make up to 1 month in advance. Cover and refrigerate.

CAJUN SEASONING

MAKES ½ CUP
2 tbsp white peppercorns
2 tbsp black peppercorns
2 tbsp cayenne pepper
1 tbsp garlic powder
1 tbsp onion powder
2 tsp dried thyme
1 tsp dry mustard powder
½ tsp ground fennel
½ tsp dried oregano
¼ tsp ground cumin

Grind ingredients together (see page 161). Use 1 tbsp for 4 servings of meat. Rub steak up to 6 hours in advance of grilling, pork ribs up to 1 day in advance, shrimp up to 2 hours in advance, fish up to 30 minutes in advance, and chicken breasts up to 6 hours in advance.

THINK AHEAD
Make up to 3 months in advance. Store in an airtight container at room temperature.

CAJUN SEASONING

ACHIOTE SEASONING

CAROLINA HONEY GLAZE

ACHIOTE SEASONING

MAKES ½ CUP

3 tbsp annatto seeds
2 tbsp dried oregano
2 tbsp cumin seeds
1 tbsp coriander seeds
1 tbsp black peppercorns
6 cloves
1 tbsp ground allspice
½ tbsp ground cinnamon

Grind the annatto seeds in a spice grinder until reduced to a powder. Toast oregano, cumin, coriander, peppercorns, and cloves (see page 161). Let cool. Add toasted spices, allspice, and cinnamon to annatto and grind together to form a powder. Use 2 tbsp per 4 servings of meat. Rub on to pork chops up to 4 hours in advance of grilling, shrimp up to 2 hours in advance, fish up to 30 minutes in advance, and chicken wings up to 8 hours in advance.

THINK AHEAD
Make up to 3 months in advance. Store in an airtight container at room temperature.

CHARMOULA

MAKES ⅔ CUP

1 handful flat-leaf parsley leaves
1 handful cilantro leaves
4 garlic cloves, crushed
1 tsp paprika
1 tsp ground cumin
½ tsp ground coriander
¼ tsp cayenne pepper
2 tbsp fresh lemon juice
2 tbsp olive oil

Place parsley, cilantro, garlic, paprika, cumin, coriander, cayenne, lemon juice, and oil in a food processor or blender; pulse to a paste. Use 1 recipe for 4 servings of meat. Use to marinate lamb up to 1 day in advance of grilling, chicken breasts up to 6 hours in advance, shrimp up to 2 hours in advance, and fish up to 30 minutes in advance.

THINK AHEAD
Make up to 3 days in advance. Cover and refrigerate.

RECADO ROJO

MAKES ½ CUP

3 tbsp achiote seasoning (see left)
6 garlic cloves, crushed
3 tbsp orange or pineapple juice
2 tbsp red wine vinegar
1 tbsp olive oil
1 tbsp honey

Combine seasoning, garlic, juice, vinegar, oil, and honey. Use to marinate pork chops up to 8 hours in advance of grilling, chicken breasts up to 4 hours in advance, shrimp up to 2 hours in advance, and fish up to 30 minutes in advance.

THINK AHEAD
Make up to 1 day in advance. Cover and refrigerate.

CHARMOULA

RECADO ROJO

SPICY JERK RUB

MAKES 1½ CUPS

6 scallions, chopped
2 scotch bonnet chiles or
  3 jalapeños, seeded and chopped
2 tbsp grated fresh ginger
4 garlic cloves, crushed
1 medium onion, chopped
1 tsp ground allspice
1 tsp dried thyme
¼ tsp cinnamon
¼ tsp grated nutmeg
2 tsp salt
1 tsp black pepper
1 tbsp rum
1 tbsp cider vinegar
1 tbsp peanut oil

Place scallions, chiles, ginger, garlic, onion, allspice, thyme, cinnamon, nutmeg, salt, pepper, rum, vinegar, and oil in a food processor or blender; pulse to a paste. Use 1 recipe per 4 servings. Rub on to meat just before grilling.

THINK AHEAD
Make up to 1 day in advance. Cover and refrigerate.

JAMAICAN JERK SEASONING

MAKES ½ CUP

2 tbsp onion powder
1 tbsp dried chives
1 tbsp dried thyme
1 tbsp ground allspice
1 tbsp salt
1 tbsp dark brown sugar
2 tsp black pepper
2 tsp cayenne pepper
2 tsp garlic powder
½ tsp grated nutmeg
½ tsp ground cinnamon

Combine onion powder, chives, thyme, allspice, salt, sugar, black pepper, cayenne pepper, garlic powder, nutmeg, and cinnamon. Use 2 tbsp per 4 servings. Rub on to pork chops up to 4 hours in advance of grilling and chicken wings up to 8 hours in advance

THINK AHEAD
Make up to 3 months in advance. Store in an airtight container at room temperature.

SPICY JERK RUB

GARAM MASALA

JAMAICAN JERK SEASONING

GARAM MASALA

MAKES ½ CUP

3 tbsp cardamom pods
2½ tbsp cumin seeds
2 tbsp coriander seeds
1½ tbsp black peppercorns
1 tbsp cloves
2 tsp ground cinnamon
1 tsp grated nutmeg

Lightly crush cardamom pods. Discard skins and reserve seeds. Toast cardamom seeds, cumin, coriander, peppercorns, and cloves (see page 161). Let cool. Crush toasted spices to a powder (see page 161). Blend with cinnamon and nutmeg. Use 2 tbsp per 4 servings. Rub on to pork chops up to 8 hours in advance of grilling, chicken breasts up to 4 hours in advance, shrimp up to 2 hours in advance and fish up to 30 minutes in advance.

THINK AHEAD
Make up to 3 months in advance. Store in an airtight container at room temperature.

SPICY TANDOORI MIX

MAKES 3½ TBSP

2 tsp kashmiri or other red chili powder
1 tbsp paprika
2 tbsp garam masala

Combine chili powder, paprika, and garam masala. Use 1 recipe per 4 servings. Rub on to lamb up to 1 day in advance of grilling, shrimp up to 2 hours in advance, fish up to 30 minutes in advance, and chicken breasts, wings and drumsticks up to 6 hours in advance.

JERKED HONEY RUM GLAZE

MAKES ½ CUP

1 tsp jerk seasoning
¼ cup honey
2 tsp dark rum

Combine seasoning, honey, and rum. Brush on to meat just before and during grilling.

THINK AHEAD
Make up to 1 month in advance. Cover and refrigerate.

SPICY TANDOORI MIX

JERKED HONEY RUM GLAZE

MARINATING

Always cover food tightly while marinating.
• The more completely the food is coated with a marinade, the quicker the flavoring process.
• If marinating in a dish, press plastic wrap directly on to the food in order to expel any air.
• A resealable plastic bag or oven roasting bag works very well to coat and seal food completely in a marinade.

Always use nonreactive containers for marinating.
• Choose glass, Pyrex, ceramic, stainless steel, and plastic.
• Never use aluminum, foil, cast iron, or copper.

Never marinate foods beyond the recommended time.
• The idea is to achieve taste without toughness.
• If you overmarinate, what you may gain in flavor, you'll sacrifice in texture, since some acidic marinades begin to break meat down if it is left too long in a mix.

Always shake excess flavor mixes off food before cooking.
• Oil that drips on to the coals causes flare-ups, and flare-ups give you burned, not flame-kissed, food.

Never mix raw and cooked.
• Don't put grilled food back in the same dish that you used for marinating. Bacteria will still be in the raw juices left behind in the dish, so be sure to use a clean dish for cooked food.

1 Heavy plastic bags
2 Glass bowl
3 Glass dish
4 Plastic tray
5 Basting brush

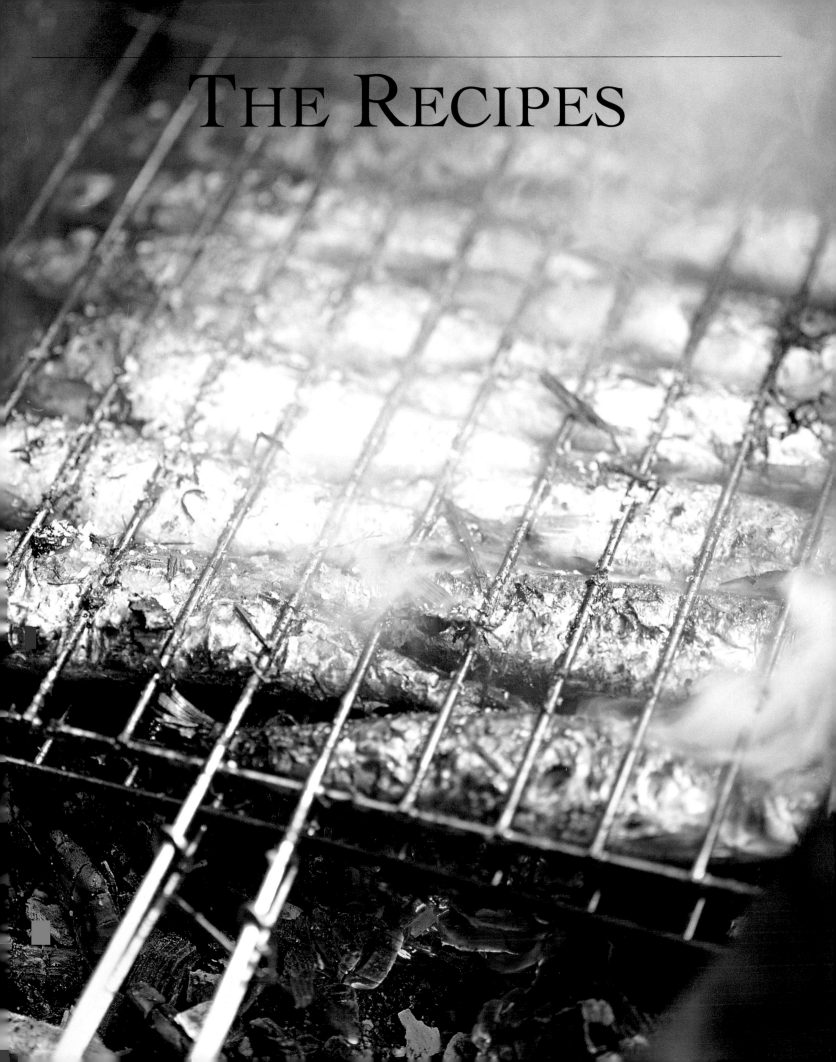

THE RECIPES

Meat on the Grill

WHAT TO GRILL

Always choose beef that is liberally marbled with fat. We recommend buying steaks from the tenderloin, loin, sirloin, or top round. Beef tastes best when cooked briefly and quickly over a high heat. This method yields succulent, juicy results.

GETTING IT READY

Well-marbled beef needs only a light brush of oil before grilling. To prevent flare-ups, trim outer fat and shake off excess marinade before placing meat on the grill.

PUTTING IT ON

To achieve professional-looking, crisscross markings on a steak, place it onto the grill until grill markings are clearly visible across the underside of meat, about 1 minute. Rotate the steak through 60° (the angle between 12 and 2 o'clock) and leave to sear 1 minute more. Turn meat over and repeat this on the opposite side.

TAKING IT OFF

Use your finger to touch test for doneness. The meat should feel soft, firm and juicy to the touch (see page 13).

When using a meat thermometer, beef should read for 150°F for medium rare and 170°F for well done.

RESTING

For juicy, tender beef, always allow meat to relax and juices to settle inside the meat before serving. Cover loosely with foil to keep warm and let stand for 5 minutes.

FINAL FLAVORING

Salting beef before cooking draws out the flavorful juices and toughens the flesh. Always add seasoning at the last minute but be sure not to forget before serving.

CHARGRILLED SIRLOIN STEAK WITH GARLIC PARSLEY BUTTER

SERVES 4

4 - 8oz sirloin steaks, 1 inch thick
1 tbsp melted butter
1 tsp black pepper
salt
4 - ½-inch slices garlic parsley butter (see page 140)

Brush steaks with melted butter. Sprinkle with pepper. Grill according to instructions below. Sprinkle with salt and let rest for 5 minutes. Serve warm, topped with garlic parsley butter.

OUTDOOR
Grill over hot coals for 3 minutes per side for rare, 4 minutes per side for medium rare, 6 minutes per side for well done.

INDOOR
Preheat a ridged cast-iron grill pan over high heat. Cook for 3 minutes per side for rare, 4 minutes per side for medium rare, 6 minutes per side for well done.

COOKS' NOTE
Any of the flavored butters on pages 140–141—blue cheese, black olive, or cilantro chili—would be delicious melted over this succulent steak.

CHARGRILLED T-BONE STEAK WITH CHIMI CHURRI SAUCE

SERVES 4
2 - 1½ lb T-bone or porterhouse steaks, 1 inch thick
1 tbsp olive oil
1 tsp black pepper
salt
1 recipe chimi churri sauce (see page 135)

Drizzle steaks with oil. Sprinkle with pepper. Grill according to instructions below.
Sprinkle with salt. Let rest 5 minutes. To serve, cut around the bone to release the meat.
Cut the meat across the grain into ¼-inch slices. Serve hot with chimi churri sauce.

OUTDOOR
Grill over hot coals for 6 minutes per side for rare,
8 minutes per side for medium rare, 12 minutes per
side for well done.

INDOOR
Preheat a ridged cast-iron grill pan over high heat.
Cook for 6 minutes per side for rare, 8 minutes per
side for medium rare, 12 minutes per side for well done.

CHARGRILLED TENDERLOIN STEAK WITH SALSA VERDE

SERVES 4

4 - 6oz tenderloin steaks, 2 inches thick
1 tbsp olive oil
1 tsp black pepper
salt
1 recipe salsa verde (see page 134)

ESSENTIAL EQUIPMENT
kitchen string

Tie a piece of string around the middle of each steak to ensure a neat shape and even cooking. Rub steaks with oil and pepper. Grill according to instructions below. Sprinkle with salt and let rest for 5 minutes. Cut string and remove. Serve warm, topped with salsa verde.

OUTDOOR
Grill over hot coals for 3 minutes per side for rare, 4 minutes per side for medium rare, 6 minutes per side for well done.

INDOOR
Preheat a ridged cast-iron grill pan over high heat. Cook for 3 minutes per side for rare, 4 minutes per side for medium rare, 6 minutes per side for well done.

SESAME SOY SKEWERED STEAKS

SERVES 4

8 - 2oz tenderloin steaks,
  1 inch thick
4 scallions

2 tbsp fresh grated ginger
3 garlic cloves, crushed
1 tsp crushed red pepper flakes
½ tsp black pepper
1 tbsp sesame oil
2 tsp packed brown sugar
6 tbsp soy sauce
1 tbsp rice vinegar or medium dry
  sherry
1 tbsp sesame seeds

ESSENTIAL EQUIPMENT
8 - 10-inch presoaked bamboo skewers

Place 2 steaks side by side on a tray.
Push one skewer diagonally through
both steaks. Push a second skewer
diagonally, in the opposite direction to
the first skewer, to secure the 2 steaks
together, forming a cross with the
2 skewers. Thread the end of a scallion
onto the pointed end of one skewer.
Thread the other end of the scallion
onto the pointed end of the second
skewer. Repeat with remaining steaks,
skewers, and scallions.
Combine ginger, garlic, crushed red
pepper flakes, pepper, oil, sugar, soy
sauce, vinegar or sherry, and sesame
seeds in a bowl. Pour mixture over
skewered steaks. Cover and refrigerate
for 30 minutes. Grill according to
instructions below. Serve hot.

OUTDOOR
Grill over medium-hot
coals for 3 minutes per
side for rare, 4 minutes
per side for medium-
rare, 6 minutes per side
for well done.

INDOOR
Preheat broiler. Broil for
3 minutes per side for
rare, 4 minutes per
side for medium-rare,
6 minutes per side for
well done.

THINK AHEAD
Skewer and marinate steaks up to 8 hours in
advance. Cover and refrigerate.

SPICED BEEF FAJITAS WITH SALSA FRESCA AND GUACAMOLE

SERVES 4

FOR MARINADE

2 garlic cloves, crushed
½ tsp crushed red pepper flakes
½ tsp ground cumin
½ tsp dried oregano
¼ tsp ground allspice
2 tbsp Mexican beer
1 tbsp olive oil

1lb skirt or flank steak

FOR GUACAMOLE

2 fresh green chiles, seeded and
  finely chopped
2 tbsp finely chopped cilantro leaves
¼ cup fresh lime juice
2 medium avocados, peeled, pitted,
  and chopped
salt, black pepper
4 flour tortillas
salt, black pepper
1 handful shredded lettuce
1 recipe salsa fresca (see page 133)
½ cup sour cream

OUTDOOR
Grill over hot coals for 5 minutes per side for rare, 7 minutes per side for medium rare, 10 minutes per side for well done. Warm tortillas by setting directly over grill for 30 seconds each side.

INDOOR
Preheat a ridged cast-iron grill pan over high heat. Cook for 5 minutes per side for rare, 7 minutes per side for medium rare, 10 minutes per side for well done. Warm tortillas by placing in broiler pan for 30 seconds each side.

THINK AHEAD
Marinate beef up to 1 day in advance. Cover and refrigerate. Make guacamole up to 1 day in advance. Cover tightly with plastic wrap, pressing on the guacamole to prevent contact with air, and refrigerate.

For marinade, combine garlic, red pepper flakes, cumin, oregano, allspice, beer, and oil. Add steak and turn to coat. Cover and refrigerate for 1 hour. For guacamole, combine chiles, cilantro, lime juice, and avocado. Mash with a potato masher until well combined but still chunky. Add salt and pepper to taste. Cover and refrigerate. Grill steak according to instructions at upper right. Let stand for 5 minutes before carving on the diagonal into ½-inch slices. Warm tortillas according to instructions opposite. Place steak slices on warmed tortillas. Sprinkle with salt and pepper. Top with lettuce, salsa fresca, guacamole, and sour cream. Roll up and serve hot.

HUNGARIAN SPICED BEEF SKEWERS WITH SOUR CREAM

SERVES 4

1lb ground chuck steak
1 onion, grated
4 garlic cloves, crushed
2 tsp paprika
1 tsp dried marjoram
1 tsp ground caraway
1 tsp black pepper
2 tsp salt
salt and black pepper
⅔ cup sour cream
1 recipe chargrilled garlic potato
   slices (see page 120), optional

ESSENTIAL EQUIPMENT
8 - 10-inch presoaked bamboo skewers

Place ground steak, onion, garlic, paprika, marjoram, caraway, pepper, and salt in a food processor; pulse until combined. Divide into 8 equal-sized portions. With wet hands, mold each portion around a skewer, shaping it into a sausage, about 8 inches long. Grill according to instructions below. Sprinkle with salt and pepper. Serve hot with sour cream and chargrilled garlic potato slices, optional.

OUTDOOR
Grill over medium-hot coals, turning every 2 minutes, until well browned but still juicy and slightly pink inside, 8–10 minutes.

INDOOR
Preheat broiler. Broil, turning every 2 minutes, until well browned but still juicy and slightly pink inside, 8–10 minutes.

THINK AHEAD
Prepare and skewer satays up to 1 day in advance. Cover with plastic wrap and refrigerate.

COOKS' NOTE
If you can find it, use Hungarian paprika, which is superior to Spanish paprika. It has a sweet, sun-dried flavor and a bright color.

CILANTRO BEEF SATAYS WITH HONEY TAMARIND GLAZE

SERVES 4

1lb ground chuck steak
2 tbsp grated
  fresh ginger
2 garlic cloves, crushed
1 onion, grated
1 handful cilantro leaves
1 tsp ground coriander

1 tsp ground turmeric
1 tsp chili powder
½ tsp ground cumin
½ tsp ground cardamom
2 tsp salt
½ tsp black pepper

FOR GLAZE
1 tbsp grated fresh ginger
1 garlic clove, crushed
1½ tbsp tamarind paste
1½ tbsp honey

salt, black pepper

ESSENTIAL EQUIPMENT
8 - 14-inch flat metal skewers

Place ground steak, ginger, garlic, onion, cilantro, ground coriander, turmeric, chili powder, cumin, cardamom, salt, and pepper in a food processor; pulse until combined. Divide into 8 equal-sized portions. With wet hands, mold each portion around a skewer, shaping it into a sausage, about 8 inches long.

For glaze, combine ginger, garlic, tamarind, and honey. Grill according to instructions below. Sprinkle with salt and pepper. Serve hot.

OUTDOOR
Grill over medium-hot coals, brushing with glaze, turning every 2 minutes, until well browned but still juicy and slightly pink inside, 8–10 minutes.

INDOOR
Preheat broiler. Brush with glaze and broil, turning every 2 minutes, until well browned but still juicy and slightly pink inside, 8–10 minutes.

THINK AHEAD
Prepare and skewer satays and make glaze up to 1 day in advance. Cover each with plastic wrap and refrigerate.

COOKS' NOTE
Dark, shiny tamarind paste—sometimes referred to as concentrate—has a refreshing, sharp citrus flavor. It is usually available from Asian and Middle-Eastern stores or from mail order sources (see page 167). If you can't find it, use tamarind pulp. For this recipe, dissolve 1 tbsp pulp in 1 tbsp boiling water, then cool and strain before using.

BEST BURGER WITH BLUE CHEESE BUTTER

SERVES 4

1lb ground chuck steak
2 tsp salt
1 tsp black pepper

4 - ½-inch slices blue cheese butter
(see page 140)
4 sesame hamburger buns, halved

Combine ground steak with salt and pepper. Divide into 4 equal-sized pieces and gently shape into 4 burgers about 1 inch thick. Grill burgers and warm buns according to instructions below. Top burgers with butter and serve hot in sesame buns.

OUTDOOR
Grill over hot coals for 3 minutes per side for rare, 4 minutes per side for medium rare, 5 minutes per side for well done. Place buns cut side down on grill until warm and lightly golden, 1 minute.

INDOOR
Preheat a ridged cast-iron grill pan over high heat. Cook for 3 minutes per side for rare, 4 minutes per side for medium rare, 5 minutes per side for well done. Place buns cut side down on grill pan until warm and lightly golden, 1 minute.

THINK AHEAD
Shape burgers up to 1 day in advance. Cover with plastic wrap and refrigerate.

COOKS' NOTE
Overhandling the meat when shaping will result in a tough, dry burger. To guarantee a juicy burger, handle the meat as little as possible.

BEST BURGER VARIATIONS
HERBED BURGER
Add 2 tsp fresh thyme leaves or 1 tsp dried thyme, 1 crushed garlic clove, and 1 tbsp finely chopped onion to the ground steak. Serve with garlic parsley butter (see page 140) in place of blue cheese butter.

SPICY BURGER
Add ½ tsp tabasco, 1 tbsp Worcestershire sauce, and 1 tsp Dijon mustard to the ground steak. Serve with cilantro chilli butter (see page 140) in place of blue cheese butter.

WHAT TO GRILL

Small, lean, and tender cuts, such as chops and ribs, will stay moist during cooking if they are marinated before and basted well during grilling. Larger cuts need to be cut into strips or cubes, and skewered. It is important for pork to be completely cooked through. Sausages are ideal for the grill, as there is plenty of evenly distributed fat to keep the meat moist while cooking.

GETTING IT READY

Trim off excess fat to avoid flare-ups. Unlike lamb and beef, the fat surrounds pork meat rather than marbling it, so to achieve meat which is cooked through but still juicy, pork should be marinated or brushed with oil before going on the grill.

TAKING IT OFF

Pork should be cooked until the internal temperature reaches 150°F. The meat should be opaque throughout but still moist.

RESTING

For juicy, tender pork, always allow meat to relax and juices to settle inside the meat before serving. Cover loosely with foil to keep warm, and let stand for 5 minutes.

FINAL FLAVORING

Salting pork before cooking draws out the flavorful juices and toughens the flesh. Always add seasoning at the last minute, but be sure not to forget.

MEXICAN SPICED PORK CHOPS WITH PINEAPPLE LIME SALSA

SERVES 4

4 pork chops, cut 1 inch thick
4 garlic cloves, crushed
1 tsp dried oregano
1 tsp ground cumin
½ tsp ground coriander
½ tsp black pepper
¼ tsp ground cinnamon

2 tbsp red wine vinegar
3 tbsp orange juice
1 tbsp honey
1 tbsp olive oil
salt, black pepper
1 recipe pineapple lime salsa
  (see page 134)

Trim off excess fat from the chops. With scissors, cut snips through the remaining fat at 1½-inch intervals. Combine garlic, oregano, cumin, coriander, black pepper, cinnamon, vinegar, orange juice, honey, and oil. Pour mixture over chops, turning several times to coat thoroughly. Cover and refrigerate for 4 hours. Grill according to instructions below. Sprinkle with salt and pepper. Serve hot with pineapple lime salsa.

OUTDOOR
Grill over medium-hot coals until there is no trace of pink near the bone but the pork is still juicy, 8–10 minutes per side.

INDOOR
Preheat a ridged cast-iron grill pan over high heat. Cook until there is no trace of pink near the bone but the pork is still juicy, 8–10 minutes per side.

THINK AHEAD
Marinate pork up to 1 day in advance. Cover and refrigerate.

ROSEMARY PEPPERED PORK CHOPS

SERVES 4

4 pork chops, cut 1 inch thick
4 garlic cloves
2 tbsp whole black peppercorns
3 tbsp fresh rosemary leaves
or 1 tbsp dried rosemary
1 tsp fennel seeds
¼ tsp crushed red pepper flakes
1 tbsp fresh lemon juice
3 tbsp olive oil
lemon wedges

Trim off excess fat from the chop. With scissors, cut snips through the remaining fat at 1½-inch intervals. Place garlic, peppercorns, rosemary, fennel seeds, red pepper flakes, lemon juice, and oil in a food processor or blender; pulse to a coarse paste. Rub the paste over both sides of the chops. Grill according to instructions below. Sprinkle with salt. Serve hot with lemon wedges.

OUTDOOR
Grill over medium-hot coals until there is no trace of pink near the bone but the pork is still juicy, 8-10 minutes per side.

INDOOR
Preheat a ridged cast-iron grill pan over high heat. Cook until there is no trace of pink near the bone but the pork is still juicy, 8–10 minutes per side.

THINK AHEAD
Rub pork with paste up to 2 hours in advance. Cover and refrigerate.

COOKS' NOTE
Snipping the outer fat with scissors prevents the chops from curling and shrinking during cooking, allowing them to remain flat and to cook evenly.

BALSAMIC PEPPERED PORK CHOPS

SERVES 4

4 pork chops, cut 1 inch thick
4 garlic cloves
2 tbsp whole black peppercorns
1 tbsp dried thyme
¼ tsp crushed red pepper flakes
1 tbsp balsamic vinegar
3 tbsp olive oil
extra balsamic vinegar for basting

Trim off excess fat from the chop. With scissors, cut snips through the remaining fat at 1½-inch intervals. Place garlic, peppercorns, thyme, red pepper flakes, vinegar, and oil in a food processor or blender; pulse to a coarse paste. Rub the paste over both sides of the chops. Grill according to instructions below.
Serve hot.

OUTDOOR
Grill over medium-hot coals, basting with the extra balsamic vinegar, until there is no trace of pink near the bone but the pork is still juicy, 8–10 minutes per side.

INDOOR
Preheat a ridged cast-iron grill pan over high heat. Cook, basting with the extra balsamic vinegar, until there is no trace of pink near the bone but the pork is still juicy, 8–10 minutes per side.

THINK AHEAD
Rub pork with paste up to 2 hours in advance. Cover and refrigerate.

COOKS' NOTE
Snipping the outer fat with scissors prevents the chops from curling and shrinking during cooking, allowing them to remain flat and to cook evenly.

SLICING AND SKEWERING PORK TENDERLOIN
Slice the pork tenderloin against the grain of the meat into strips ¼ inch thick and about 4–6 inches long.

Lay the strips flat on a board, side by side. Thread onto 3 parallel skewers.

SWEET SOY GLAZED PORK

SERVES 4

1lb pork tenderloin, sliced and skewered (see left)	**¼ cup hoisin sauce**
⅓ cup soy sauce	**3 tbsp medium dry sherry**
3 tbsp tomato ketchup	**3 tbsp honey**
	3 tbsp packed brown sugar

ESSENTIAL EQUIPMENT
3 - 14-inch flat metal skewers

Combine soy sauce, ketchup, hoisin, sherry, honey, and sugar. Set aside 6 tbsp of the glaze Spread remaining mixture over both sides of the pork skewers. Grill according to instructions below. Serve hot with the remaining glaze drizzled.

OUTDOOR
Grill over medium-hot coals until pork is opaque but still juicy, 3 minutes per side.

INDOOR
Preheat broiler. Broil until pork is opaque but still juicy, 3 minutes per side.

THINK AHEAD
Marinate pork up to 4 hours in advance. Cover and refrigerate.

SPICY PORK SATAY

SERVES 4

**1lb pork tenderloin,
  sliced and skewered
  (see page 46)**
2 lemon grass stalks
1 tbsp grated fresh ginger
2 garlic cloves, crushed
1 onion
2 tsp ground fennel
2 tsp ground cumin

2 tsp ground coriander
1 tsp turmeric
1 tbsp fresh lime juice
1 tbsp peanut oil
salt, black pepper
**1 recipe spicy peanut sauce
  (see page 136) to serve**

ESSENTIAL EQUIPMENT
12 - 10-inch presoaked bamboo skewers

Remove and discard the tough outer skin from the lemon grass
stalks and roughly chop. Place lemon grass, ginger, garlic,
onion, fennel, cumin, coriander, turmeric, lime juice, and oil
in a food processor or blender; pulse to form a smooth paste.
Spread paste over both sides of the pork skewers. Cover
and refrigerate for 4 hours. Grill according to instructions at
upper right. Sprinkle with salt and pepper. Serve hot with
spicy peanut sauce.

OUTDOOR
Grill over medium-hot coals until pork
is opaque but still juicy, 3 minutes
per side.

INDOOR
Preheat broiler. Broil until pork
is opaque but still juicy, 3 minutes
per side.

THINK AHEAD
Marinate pork up to 1 day in advance. Cover and refrigerate.

COOKS' NOTE
For maximum flavor, be sure to freshly toast and crush all the spices
(see page 161).

GARLIC MUSTARD PORK SKEWERS

SERVES 4

2 garlic cloves, crushed	2 tbsp grainy mustard
2 tbsp Worcestershire sauce	2 tbsp Dijon mustard
2 tbsp soy sauce	¼ tbsp runny honey
4 tbsp tomato ketchup	1lb pork tenderloin,
1 tbsp tomato paste	sliced and skewered
1 tsp tabasco	(see page 46)
2 tbsp cider vinegar	
2 tsp paprika	

ESSENTIAL EQUIPMENT
3 - 14-inch flat metal skewers

Combine garlic, Worcestershire sauce, soy sauce, tomato ketchup, tomato paste, tabasco, vinegar, paprika, mustards, and honey. Set aside ⅓ cup of the glaze. Spread remaining glaze over both sides of the pork skewers. Grill according to instructions below. Serve hot with the remaining glaze.

OUTDOOR
Grill over medium-hot coals until pork is opaque but still juicy, 3 minutes per side.

INDOOR
Preheat broiler. Broil until pork is opaque but still juicy, 3 minutes per side.

THINK AHEAD
Marinate pork up to 4 hours in advance. Cover and refrigerate.

COOKS' NOTE
If you can find it, use smoked paprika for this recipe. Smoked paprika is a specialty paprika from Spain. Unlike other paprikas, the peppers are not sun-dried, but oak-smoked, before being ground. This gives it a deep, rusty red color and a distinctive smoky flavor. Smoked paprika is available from mail order and specialty stores (see page 167).

THAI SWEET & SOUR RIBS

SERVES 4
4lbs pork spareribs
1 red onion, finely chopped
2 garlic cloves, crushed
1 tbsp grated fresh ginger
1 tbsp peanut oil
½ cup pineapple juice
2 tbsp fish sauce
¼ cup tomato paste
¼ cup fresh lime juice
2 tbsp honey
⅓ cup Thai sweet chili sauce

Separate ribs by slicing between the bones with a large knife or cleaver. Simmer separated ribs in large pan of salted water until just tender, about 30 minutes. Drain. Rinse under cold running water and drain again. Let cool completely. Place onion, garlic, ginger, and oil in a small pan. Stir fry over medium heat until softened, 5–10 minutes. Add pineapple juice, fish sauce, tomato paste, lime juice, honey, and 2 tbsp sweet chili sauce. Bring to a boil. Simmer gently until thick, 10 minutes. Let cool completely. Brush the sweet sour mixture over the ribs. Grill according to instructions below, basting with the remaining chili sauce throughout. Serve hot.

OUTDOOR
Grill over medium-hot coals, turning frequently and basting, until brown and crusty, 15 minutes.

INDOOR
Preheat broiler. Broil, removing from under the broiler every 5 minutes to baste, until brown and crusty, 15 minutes.

THINK AHEAD
Precook the ribs up to 1 day in advance. Cool completely. Cover with plastic wrap and refrigerate. Make glaze up to 1 day in advance. Cover and refrigerate.

COOKS' NOTE
Precook the ribs in simmering water to remove the layer of outer fat. This not only prevents flare-ups during cooking, but allows the rib meat to stay tender and juicy inside and crispy on the outside.

RIB VARIATION
SPICED HOISIN RIBS

Omit all ingredients for the sweet sour mixture. Combine instead ½ cup hoisin sauce, ½ tsp Chinese five-spice, 4 crushed garlic cloves, 2 tbsp grated fresh ginger, 2 tbsp medium dry sherry, ¼ cup soy sauce, 2 tbsp Chinese hot chili sauce, and ½ cup packed brown sugar. Reserve 2 tbsp hoisin mixture for basting. Brush remaining mixture over ribs. Grill according to recipe above.

MAKING SAUSAGES

Run water through the casings to check for any holes or tears.

Gather casing up onto the tip until you reach the end of the casing.

Twist the top of the bag until the filling is visible in the tip, to clear any air pockets before you begin.

Gently squeeze the bag so that the casing fills evenly and forms a long sausage.

Prick all over with a toothpick to prevent the sausage from bursting during cooking.

COOKS' NOTE
Most butchers will sell you sausage casing if you give them some advance notice. The casing should come packed in salt.

TOULOUSE SAUSAGES

SERVES 4
1lb-piece boneless slab bacon
2 tsp salt
1 tsp black pepper
⅓ cup plus 2 tbsp cold water
3ft sausage casings

ESSENTIAL EQUIPMENT
Piping bag fitted with large plain tip, hinged grill rack or 2 flat metal skewers

Remove the rind from the bacon and cut into 1in cubes. Place bacon cubes, salt, pepper, and water in a food processor; pulse until the ground pork begins to form a ball.

Rinse the casings under cold running water and soak in a large bowl of cold water. This will remove excess salt and make the casings more pliable. Run water through casings to check for any holes or tears. Insert the piping tip into one end of the casing. Gather casing up onto the tip until you reach the other end of the casing. Fill the piping bag with sausagemeat. Twist the top of the bag until the filling is visible in the tip. Gently squeeze the top of the piping bag so that the casing fills evenly with the sausagemeat and forms a long sausage. Prick the finished sausage all over with a toothpick. See illustrations at left for guidance.

For outdoor grilling, place the coiled sausage in a hinged grill rack, if using. Alternatively, and for indoor cooking, secure by pushing 2 skewers crossing each other through the coiled sausage. Grill according to instructions below. Serve hot.

OUTDOOR
Grill over medium-hot coals until browned and cooked through, 8–10 minutes per side.

INDOOR
Preheat broiler. Broil until browned and cooked through, 8–10 minutes per side.

THINK AHEAD
Make sausages up to 1 day in advance. Cover with plastic wrap and refrigerate.

SAUSAGE VARIATIONS

GARLIC SAUSAGES

Add 12 large garlic cloves, crushed, to the food processor with the bacon cubes, salt, pepper, and water. Prepare and stuff casing according to recipe above.

SPICY SAUSAGES

Add 2 tsp paprika, 1 seeded and finely chopped fresh red chile and 4 crushed garlic cloves in the food processor with the bacon cubes, salt, pepper, and water. Prepare and stuff casing according to recipe above.

PERFECT MEAT FOR THE GRILL

Lamb is the original inspiration for the Mediterranean's great tradition of outdoor grilling and feasting. The meat is liberally and evenly marbled with fat, making it the ideal meat for the grill.

GETTING IT READY

Cut off excess fat to avoid flare-ups. Pull off the thin transparent membrane surrounding the meat and trim off any connective tissue.

PUTTING IT ON

Remove small cuts from the refrigerator 30 minutes, and large cuts 45 minutes, before grilling. To avoid flare-ups, shake off excess marinade before placing on the grill.

TAKING IT OFF

The surface of lamb cooks much faster than the interior, which results in a crisp, browned exterior with juicy meat inside. Use your finger to touch test for doneness. The meat should feel soft, firm and juicy to the touch (see page 13). When using a meat thermometer, lamb should read 150°F for rare, and 170°F for well done.

RESTING

For juicy, tender lamb, and in particular for large cuts, allow meat to relax and the juices to settle inside the meat before carving. Cover loosely with foil to keep warm and let stand for 10 minutes.

FINAL FLAVORING

Salting lamb before cooking draws out the flavorful juices and toughens the flesh. Always add seasoning at the last minute, but be sure not to forget before serving.

BONING AND HERB-SKEWERING CHOPS
Trim off excess fat from chops. Cut around the bone to release the meat.

Pull the flap round each chop to make a round shape. With a small, sharp knife make a slit through the chop, passing first through the flap. Push the sharp end of the rosemary sprig through the slit to secure.

THINK AHEAD
Bone and skewer chops up to 1 day in advance. Cover and refrigerate.

COOKS' NOTE
You can use a bamboo or metal skewer instead of a rosemary sprig.

ROSEMARY LAMB CHOPS WITH MUSTARD MINT DRESSING

SERVES 4

8 4-inch rosemary sprigs
8 lamb loin chops, boned (see left)
1 garlic clove, crushed
2 tsp black pepper
1 tbsp balsamic vinegar
1 tbsp olive oil
salt

FOR DRESSING
1 tbsp Dijon mustard
2 tbsp finely chopped fresh mint leaves
3 tbsp fresh lemon juice
⅓ cup olive oil
salt, black pepper

For skewers, strip the leaves from the rosemary sprigs, leaving a few leaves at one end of each stalk. Sharpen the other end to a point with a knife. Use sprigs to skewer lamb (see left). Combine garlic, pepper, vinegar, and oil. Rub onto both sides of lamb. Cover and refrigerate for 30 minutes.

For dressing, combine mustard, mint, and lemon juice. Gradually whisk in oil to make a thick dressing. Add salt and pepper to taste. Grill skewered lamb according to instructions below. Sprinkle with salt and pepper. Top with dressing and serve hot.

OUTDOOR
Grill over hot coals for 3 minutes per side for medium rare, 5 minutes per side for well done.

INDOOR
Preheat a ridged cast-iron grill pan over high heat. Cook for 3 minutes per side for medium rare, 5 minutes per side for well done.

THINK AHEAD
Skewer and rub lamb up to 1 day in advance. Cover tightly with plastic wrap and refrigerate. Make dressing up to 4 hours in advance. Cover and store at room temperature.

BUTTERFLIED LEG OF LAMB WITH ANCHOVY, PROSCIUTTO, AND PARSLEY

SERVES 4–6

FOR PASTE
2oz prosciutto
6 anchovy fillets
1 handful flat-leaf parsley leaves
2 garlic cloves
1 tbsp balsamic vinegar

ESSENTIAL EQUIPMENT
2 - 14-inch flat metal skewers

4lb leg of lamb, butterflied
 (see left)
2 tbsp balsamic vinegar for drizzling
salt, black pepper
1 recipe salsa verde (see page 134)
 to serve, optional

Place prosciutto, anchovies, parsley, garlic, and vinegar in a food processor or blender; pulse to a smooth paste. Place lamb skin side down. With a sharp knife, cut ½-inch deep slits across the lamb about 2 inches apart. Push the paste deep into the slits. Insert skewers diagonally from opposite corners through butterflied lamb. Grill according to instructions below, drizzling balsamic vinegar on both sides during cooking. Remove to a board, cover with foil, and leave to rest for 10 minutes before slicing. Sprinkle with salt and pepper. Serve warm with salsa verde, optional.

OUTDOOR
Grill over medium-hot coals, turning once, for 15 minutes per side for medium rare or 20 minutes per side for well done.

INDOOR
Preheat broiler. Arrange lamb on a wire rack over a broiler tray. Broil, turning once, for 15 minutes per side for medium rare or 20 minutes per side for well done.

THINK AHEAD
Make paste up to 2 days in advance. Cover and refrigerate. Prepare lamb and stuff with paste up to 1 day in advance. Double wrap in plastic wrap and refrigerate. Remove from refrigerator 45 minutes before grilling.

COOKS' NOTE
Skewering the butterflied lamb helps keep the meat together and also makes it easier to move on the grill.

BUTTERFLYING LEG OF LAMB
Put the leg of lamb on a board, skin side down. Cut around the exposed bone at the wide end of the leg. Cut the bone free at the joint and detach. Cut a slit along the length of the bone to expose and loosen. Use short, shallow cuts and scrape with the knife blade to release the meat from the bone. Remove bone.
Keeping the blade of the knife horizontal, make a lengthwise slit along the thick section of the meat next to the cavity left by the leg bone. Open out the flap and spread the meat flat like a book. Make another horizontal cut into the thick meat opposite and open out flat to form a "butterfly" shape with the entire piece.

COOKS' NOTE
Butterflying is a very useful technique for preparing meat for the grill. It allows the home chef to grill a large cut of meat in a quarter of time it would take to roast it. You'll find a boned cut easier to carve with less waste.

ROLLING BUTTERFLIED LEG OF LAMB
Spread the meat evenly with seasoning and herbs. Roll up lengthwise as tightly as possible. Place roll seam-side down on a board.

Secure the roll with string. Starting in the center, tie the meat tightly at ¾-inch intervals.

Cut between the strings to make equal-sized steaks.

COOKS' NOTE
This technique transforms a leg of lamb into boneless individual portions that have all the flavor of the whole cut, but can be cooked and served with speed and ease.

LEG OF LAMB STEAKS WITH BLACK OLIVE BUTTER

SERVES 4

4lb leg of lamb, butterflied (see page 54)
1 tbsp salt
2 tsp black pepper

ESSENTIAL EQUIPMENT
kitchen string

3 tbsp stripped fresh thyme leaves
1 recipe black olive butter (see page 140)

Sprinkle the meat evenly with salt, pepper, and thyme. Roll up, secure with string and cut into steaks (see left). Grill according to instructions below. Just before removing from the grill, top each steak with a slice of black olive butter.

OUTDOOR
Grill over medium hot coals, turning once, 5 minutes per side for medium rare or 8 minutes per side for well done.

INDOOR
Preheat a ridged cast-iron-grill over high heat. Cook, turning once, 5 minutes per side for medium rare or 8 minutes per side for well done.

THINK AHEAD
Roll, stuff, and slice lamb up to 2 days in advance. Double wrap in plastic wrap and refrigerate. Remove to room temperature 20 minutes before grilling.

COOKS' NOTE
For a butter-free alternative, we suggest serving the lamb steaks with spiced chickpea sauce (see page 137) in place of the black olive butter.

BUTTERFLIED LEG OF LAMB PERSILLADE

SERVES 4–6

4lb leg of lamb, butterflied (see page 54)
1 tbsp salt
2 tsp black pepper
6 garlic cloves, sliced
2 handfuls flat-leaf parsley leaves, roughly chopped

ESSENTIAL EQUIPMENT
3 - 14-inch flat metal skewers

Follow steps in photographs at left: Prepare the butterflied lamb for stuffing by slicing it open again; sprinkle the meat evenly with salt and pepper; spread garlic and parsley over one half of the meat; fold in half and secure with skewers.
Grill according to instructions below. Remove to a cutting board, cover with foil, and let rest for 5 minutes before slicing.

OUTDOOR
Grill over medium hot coals, turning once, for 15 minutes per side for medium rare or 20 minutes per side for well done.

INDOOR
Preheat broiler. Arrange lamb on a wire rack over a broiler tray. Broil, turning once, for 15 minutes per side for medium rare or 20 minutes per side for well done.

THINK AHEAD
Slice, stuff, and skewer lamb up to 2 days in advance. Double wrap in plastic wrap and refrigerate. Remove to room temperature 45 minutes before grilling.

COOKS' NOTE
Serve with potato focaccia with thyme (see page 155) or creamy potato salad with celery and chives (see page 148).

STUFFING BUTTERFLIED LEG OF LAMB
Hold the meat firmly with the flat of your hand. Keeping the blade of the knife horizontal, slice into the thickest part of the meat again to open an additional flap for stuffing.

Sprinkle over the stuffing.

Thread the skewers through both sides of the meat to secure.

COOKS' NOTE
Here we slice a butterflied leg in half again to make a pocket for flavorful stuffing. This makes spectacular presentation that never fails to impress.

BONING SHOULDER

Place shoulder skin side down. Cut a slit along the length of the two bones to expose. Cut and scrape the meat free from the shoulder bone. Cut through the joint to free the shoulder bone.

Cut through the meat on either side of the blade bone. Scraping the bone free, pull away the blade bone from the meat.

CUBING BONELESS LAMB

Trim off excess fat. Cut the meat into 1½-inch strips.
Cut the strips into 1½-inch cubes. You will need 20 cubes for 4 servings.

THINK AHEAD
Bone and cube lamb shoulder up to 2 days in advance. Cover tightly with plastic wrap and refrigerate.

COOKS' NOTE
You need about 2lbs of lamb shoulder on the bone to yield about 1lb boneless lamb. If you prefer a leaner cut, choose boneless leg of lamb.

CORIANDER LAMB PITA WRAP

SERVES 4

1lb boneless lamb, cut into
  1½-inch cubes (see left)

FOR MARINADE
1½ tsp ground coriander
½ tsp ground cumin
¼ tsp ground allspice
¼ tsp ground cinnamon
2 tbsp fresh lemon juice
2 tbsp olive oil
1 tomato, halved

½ medium onion
2 garlic cloves

FOR WRAP
4 pita or flatbreads
1 handful shredded lettuce
4 tomatoes, cut into wedges
16 fresh mint leaves
1 recipe lemon tahini sauce
  (see page 132)
salt, black pepper

ESSENTIAL EQUIPMENT
4 - 14-inch flat metal skewers

Place coriander, cumin, allspice, cinnamon, lemon juice, oil, tomato, onion, and garlic in food processor or blender; pulse to form a thick paste. In a bowl, combine paste with lamb cubes, tossing to coat evenly. Cover and refrigerate for 2 hours. Thread lamb onto skewers. Grill according to instructions below. Split and separate each pita into 2 halves. Stack 2 pita halves cut side up. Using a fork, slide the lamb pieces from 1 skewer onto the pita. Top with a quarter of the lettuce, tomatoes, and mint. Drizzle with lemon tahini sauce. Sprinkle with salt and pepper and roll up. Repeat with remaining pita, lamb, lettuce, tomatoes, mint, and tahini sauce. Serve hot.

OUTDOOR
Grill over medium-hot coals, turning every 2 minutes, until well browned but still juicy and slightly pink inside, 8–10 minutes. Place pita halves directly on the grill until just warm, about 30 seconds per side.

INDOOR
Preheat broiler. Broil, turning every 2 minutes, until well browned but still juicy and slightly pink inside, 8–10 minutes. Briefly warm pita halves under the broiler, about 15 seconds per side.

THINK AHEAD
Marinate lamb up to 1 day in advance. Cover and refrigerate.

LAMB TIKKA MASALA

SERVES 4

1lb boneless lamb, cut into 1½-inch cubes
  (see page 58)
2 tbsp grated fresh ginger
4 garlic cloves, crushed
1 fresh green chile, seeded and finely chopped
2 tbsp finely chopped cilantro leaves
2 tbsp garam masala mix (see page 25)
1 tsp ground turmeric
2 tbsp red wine vinegar
⅔ cup Greek-style whole milk yogurt or
  sour cream
20 fresh bay leaves
20 fresh whole green chiles
salt, black pepper
4 naan or other flat bread
1 recipe cucumber yogurt raita (see page 138), optional

ESSENTIAL EQUIPMENT
4 - 14-inch flat metal skewers

Combine lamb cubes, ginger, garlic, chile, cilantro, masala mix, turmeric, vinegar, and yogurt or sour cream. Toss well to coat evenly. Cover and refrigerate for 2 hours. Thread lamb cubes, bay leaves, and chiles onto skewers. Grill lamb skewers and warm naan according to instructions below. Sprinkle with salt and pepper. Serve hot with warm naan and cucumber yogurt raita, optional.

OUTDOOR
Grill over medium-hot coals, turning every 2 minutes, until well browned but still juicy and slightly pink inside, 8–10 minutes. Warm the naan by setting directly on the grill, 1 minute per side.

INDOOR
Preheat broiler. Broil, turning every 2 minutes, until well browned but still juicy and slightly pink inside, 8–10 minutes. Briefly warm the naan under the broiler, 30 seconds per side.

THINK AHEAD
Marinate lamb cubes up to 1 day in advance. Cover and refrigerate.

SPICED COCONUT LAMB SATAYS

SERVES 4

1lb boneless lamb, cut into 1½-inch cubes
  (see page 58)
1 onion, chopped
2 garlic cloves, crushed
2 fresh red chiles, seeded and chopped
1 tbsp grated fresh ginger
1 tsp ground coriander
1 tbsp tamarind paste or fresh lime juice
3 tbsp coconut milk
1 tbsp soy sauce
1 tbsp packed brown sugar
salt, black pepper
1 recipe spicy peanut sauce (see page 136), optional

ESSENTIAL EQUIPMENT
4 - 14-inch flat metal skewers

Place onion, garlic, chiles, ginger, coriander, tamarind or lime juice, coconut milk, soy sauce, and sugar in food processor or blender; pulse to form a paste. In a bowl, combine paste with lamb cubes, tossing to coat evenly. Cover and refrigerate for 2 hours. Thread lamb onto skewers. Grill according to instructions below. Sprinkle with salt and pepper. Serve hot with spicy peanut sauce, optional.

OUTDOOR
Grill over medium-hot coals, turning every 2 minutes, until well browned but still juicy and slightly pink inside, 8–10 minutes.

INDOOR
Preheat broiler. Broil, turning every 2 minutes, until well browned but still juicy and slightly pink inside, 8–10 minutes.

THINK AHEAD
Marinate lamb up to 1 day in advance. Cover and refrigerate.

COOKS' NOTE
Dark, shiny tamarind paste— sometimes referred to as concentrate—has a refreshing, sharp citrus flavor. It is usually found in Asian and Middle-Eastern stores. If you can't find it, use tamarind pulp. For this recipe, dissolve 2 tbsp pulp in 1/4 cup boiling water, then cool and strain before using. Alternatively, use lime juice.

HONEY HARISSA KOFTE

SERVES 4

1lb ground lamb
1 onion, grated
4 garlic cloves, crushed
2 tbsp finely chopped fresh mint leaves
1 tbsp honey
1 tbsp tomato paste
3 tsp ground coriander
2 tsp ground cumin
1 tsp ground caraway seeds
1 tsp crushed red pepper flakes
1½ tsp salt
½ tsp black pepper
1 recipe radish tzatziki (see page 135), optional

ESSENTIAL EQUIPMENT
8 - 10-inch presoaked bamboo skewers

Place ground lamb, onion, garlic, mint, honey, tomato paste, coriander, cumin, caraway, red pepper flakes, salt, and pepper in a food processor; pulse until combined. Divide into 8 equal-sized portions. With wet hands, mold each portion around a skewer, shaping it into a sausage, about 6 inches long. Grill according to instructions below. Sprinkle with salt and pepper. Serve hot with radish tzatziki, optional.

OUTDOOR
Grill over medium-hot coals, turning every 2 minutes, until well browned but still juicy and slightly pink inside, 8–10 minutes.

INDOOR
Preheat broiler. Broil, turning every 2 minutes, until well browned but still juicy and slightly pink inside, 8–10 minutes.

THINK AHEAD
Prepare and skewer kofte up to 1 day in advance. Cover with plastic wrap and refrigerate.

CHARMOULA LAMB KOFTE

SERVES 4

1lb ground lamb
1 onion, grated
½ tsp black pepper
1½ tsp salt
1 recipe charmoula (see page 23)
1 recipe spiced chickpea sauce (see page 137), optional

ESSENTIAL EQUIPMENT
8 -14-inch flat metal skewers

Place lamb, onion, black pepper, salt, and charmoula in a food processor; pulse until combined. Divide into 8 equal-sized portions. With wet hands, mold each portion around a skewer, shaping it into a sausage, about 6 inches long. Grill according to instructions below. Sprinkle with salt and pepper. Serve hot with spiced chickpea sauce, optional.

OUTDOOR
Grill over medium-hot coals, turning every 2 minutes, until well browned but still juicy and slightly pink inside, 8–10 minutes.

INDOOR
Preheat broiler. Broil, turning every 2 minutes, until well browned but still juicy and slightly pink inside, 8–10 minutes.

THINK AHEAD
Prepare and skewer kofte up to 1 day in advance. Cover with plastic wrap and refrigerate.

SKEWERING AND SLASHING FILLETS

Cut the fillets into four equal-sized pieces. Thread a skewer lengthwise through the middle of each piece.

With a sharp knife, make cuts approximately 1 inch apart down the length of each skewered piece.

THINK AHEAD
Skewer and slash fillets up to 1 day in advance. Cover and refrigerate.

COOKS' NOTE
Slashing lamb ensures that the marinade will penetrate the meat completely, and that the meat will cook evenly.

SKEWERED CUMIN LAMB WITH GARLIC YOGURT SAUCE

SERVES 4

1lb boned lamb fillets,
  skewered and slashed (see left)

FOR MARINADE
2 garlic cloves, crushed
2 tbsp cumin seeds, toasted and
  roughly pounded (see page 161)
½ tsp ground coriander
½ tsp crushed red pepper flakes
1 tbsp fresh lemon juice
1 tbsp olive oil

FOR SAUCE
2 whole unpeeled garlic heads
1 tbsp olive oil
salt, black pepper
2 tsp Dijon mustard
2 tbsp balsamic vinegar
2 tbsp heavy cream
1 handful flat-leaf parsley leaves
⅔ cup Greek-style yogurt
salt, black pepper

ESSENTIAL EQUIPMENT
4 - 10-inch presoaked bamboo skewers

For marinade, combine garlic, cumin, coriander, red pepper flakes, lemon juice, and oil. Rub over skewered lamb fillets. Cover and refrigerate for 1 hour. For sauce, preheat oven to 350°F. Slice off top of both garlic heads, cutting through the tops of the cloves. Place cut-side up in oven tray. Drizzle with olive oil and sprinkle with salt and pepper. Roast until completely soft, 1 hour. Leave until cool enough to handle. Squeeze out cloves from papery skins into a food processor or blender. Add mustard, vinegar, cream, parsley, yogurt, and sour cream; pulse until smooth. Add salt and pepper to taste. Grill lamb according to instructions below. Sprinkle lamb with salt and pepper. Serve hot with the garlic yogurt sauce.

OUTDOOR
Grill over medium-hot coals, turning every 2 minutes, 8 minutes for medium rare, 12 minutes for well done.

INDOOR
Preheat a ridged cast-iron grill pan over high heat. Cook, turning every 2 minutes, 8 minutes for medium rare, 12 minutes for well done.

THINK AHEAD
Make sauce up to 1 day in advance. Cover and refrigerate. Marinate lamb up to 1 day in advance. Cover and refrigerate.

COOKS' NOTE
Spiced chickpea sauce (see page 137) or radish tzatziki (see page 135) are excellent alternatives to the garlic yogurt sauce served with this Middle-Eastern-spiced lamb dish.

SHRIMP WITH SALSA FRESCA

SERVES 4

1 recipe salsa fresca (see page 133)
1lb medium shrimp, cooked
  and peeled
2 tbsp chopped cilantro leaves

2 tbsp sour cream
salt, black pepper, tabasco
1 large bag plain, lightly salted
  tortilla chips

ESSENTIAL EQUIPMENT
heavy cast-iron skillet

Set dry pan over grill or stove as instructed below. When pan is hot, add salsa. When salsa is bubbling add shrimp and stir fry until shrimp are hot, 1 minute. Remove from heat. Stir in cilantro and cream. Add salt, pepper, and tabasco to taste. Add a handful of tortilla chips. Serve hot, with extra tortilla chips and sour cream for dipping.

OUTDOOR
On a charcoal grill, set pan over hot, flaming coals.

INDOOR
Set pan on stove over high heat.

SPICY MASALA SHRIMP

SERVES 4

¼ cup garam masala mix
  (see page 25)
1 tsp chili powder
2 tbsp paprika
2 tsp turmeric
1 tsp ground coriander
2 tsp salt
4 garlic cloves, crushed
1 tbsp grated fresh ginger
1 tbsp lemon juice
½ cup butter, melted
20 raw unpeeled large
  heads-on shrimp
lemon wedges

ESSENTIAL EQUIPMENT
20 - 10-inch presoaked bamboo skewers

Combine garam masala mix, chili powder, paprika, turmeric, coriander, salt, garlic, ginger, lemon juice, and butter to make a paste. Rub paste thoroughly into shrimp to coat evenly. Skewer each shrimp onto the end of a single skewer. Cover with plastic wrap and refrigerate for 30 minutes. Grill according to instructions below. Serve with lemon wedges.

OUTDOOR
Grill over medium-hot coals until the shell is pink and the flesh is opaque, 3 minutes per side.

INDOOR
Preheat broiler. Broil until the shell is pink and the flesh is opaque, 3 minutes per side.

THINK AHEAD
Rub shrimp with paste up to 2 hours in advance. Cover and refrigerate.

COOKS' NOTE
Use Kashmiri chili powder for an authentically Indian flavor and color. This chili powder is made from the mildly spicy and pungent chiles that are traditionally used in tandoori dishes.

SWEET SESAME SHRIMP

SERVES 4

1 tbsp sesame seeds
1 tbsp sesame oil
2 garlic cloves, crushed
1 tbsp soy sauce
1 tbsp mirin
20 raw large shrimp, peeled
lime wedges

ESSENTIAL EQUIPMENT
4 - 10-inch presoaked bamboo skewers

Combine sesame seeds, sesame oil, garlic, soy sauce, and mirin. Add shrimp and toss to coat evenly. Thread 5 shrimp onto each presoaked skewer. Cover with plastic wrap and refrigerate for 30 minutes. Grill according to instructions below. Serve with lime wedges.

OUTDOOR
Grill over medium-hot coals until the shell is pink and the flesh is opaque, 3 minutes per side.

INDOOR
Preheat broiler. Broil until the shell is pink and the flesh is opaque, 3 minutes per side.

THINK AHEAD
Marinate shrimp up to 2 hours in advance. Cover and refrigerate.

LEMON CHILI SHRIMP

SERVES 4

3 tbsp fresh lemon juice
½ tbsp Chinese hot chili sauce
1 tbsp grated fresh ginger
2 garlic cloves, crushed
2 tbsp chopped cilantro leaves
1 tbsp soy sauce
1 tbsp honey
20 raw unpeeled large shrimp

ESSENTIAL EQUIPMENT
8 - 10-inch presoaked bamboo skewers

Combine lemon juice, chili sauce, ginger, garlic, cilantro, soy sauce, and honey. Add shrimp and toss to coat evenly. Thread 5 shrimp onto parallel skewers. Repeat with remaining shrimp and skewers. Cover with plastic wrap and refrigerate for 30 minutes. Grill according to instructions below.

OUTDOOR
Grill over medium-hot coals until the shell is pink and the flesh is opaque, 3 minutes per side.

INDOOR
Preheat broiler. Broil until the shell is pink and the flesh is opaque, 3 minutes per side.

THINK AHEAD
Marinate shrimp up to 2 hours in advance. Cover and refrigerate.

SHRIMP WITH TAMARIND RECADO

SERVES 4

FOR RECADO
3 tbsp tamarind paste
1 chipotle in adobo, seeded and
finely chopped
3 garlic cloves, crushed

ESSENTIAL EQUIPMENT
4 - 10-inch presoaked bamboo skewers

1 tsp salt
1 tsp brown sugar
20 raw large shrimp, peeled
1 recipe pineapple lime salsa
(see page 134)

SHRIMP VARIATION
SPICY LIME SHRIMP

Omit tamarind recado and replace with 2 crushed garlic cloves, 1 tsp paprika, ½ tsp chili powder, 1 tbsp fresh lime juice, 1 tsp salt. Marinate, skewer and grill shrimp according to recipe at left. Serve with pineapple lime salsa or lime wedges.

For recado, combine tamarind paste, chipotle, garlic, salt, and sugar. Add shrimp and toss to coat evenly. Thread 5 shrimp onto each presoaked skewer. Cover with plastic wrap and refrigerate for 30 minutes. Grill according to instructions below. Serve with pineapple lime salsa.

OUTDOOR
Grill over medium-hot coals until the shell is pink and the flesh is opaque, 3 minutes per side.

INDOOR
Preheat broiler. Broil until the shell is pink and the flesh is opaque, 3 minutes per side.

THINK AHEAD
Marinate shrimp up to 2 hours in advance. Cover and refrigerate.

COOKS' NOTE
Dark, shiny tamarind paste—sometimes referred to as concentrate—has a refreshing, sharp citrus flavor (see page 159). It can be found in most Asian and Middle-Eastern stores. If you can't find the paste, use tamarind pulp. For this recipe, dissolve 3 tbsp pulp in 3 tbsp boiling water, then cool and strain before using.

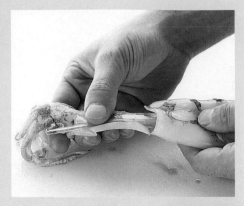

CLEANING SQUID

Pull the body from the head and tentacles. Pull out the plasticlike quill. Reserve body tube.

Cut the tentacles from the head in front of the eyes. Squeeze the "beak" from the tentacles and discard, reserving tentacles.

Peel the purple skin from the body tubes and tentacles. Wash the tubes under cold running water.

COOKS' NOTE
Cleaning squid may look daunting and messy, but it's a surprisingly quick and easy process.

BABY SQUID STUFFED WITH CILANTRO AND PICKLED GINGER

SERVES 4

12 baby squid, about 3in long, cleaned (see left)
1 tbsp shoyu (Japanese soy sauce)
1 tbsp peanut oil
½ tsp black pepper

12 pieces Japanese pickled ginger
2 tbsp cilantro leaves
2 garlic cloves, finely sliced
extra shoyu to drizzle

ESSENTIAL EQUIPMENT
24 - 10-inch presoaked bamboo skewers

Combine squid, shoyu, oil, and pepper. Toss to coat evenly.
Place 1 piece pickled ginger, a few cilantro leaves and 1 garlic slice inside each tube. Insert the tentacles into the tubes. Thread 2 skewers through each squid to secure tentacles to tubes. Grill according to instructions below. Drizzle with shoyu.
Serve hot.

OUTDOOR
Grill over medium-hot coals until just opaque, 1–2 minutes per side.

INDOOR
Preheat a ridged cast-iron grill pan over high heat. Cook until just opaque, 1–2 minutes per side.

THINK AHEAD
Prepare squid up to 2 hours in advance. Cover with plastic wrap and refrigerate.

COOKS' NOTE
If you don't have pickled ginger, you can use fresh ginger instead. Grate a 1/2-inch piece of ginger and divide evenly among squid tubes.

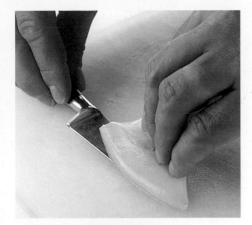

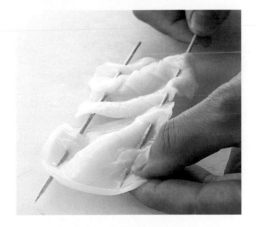

OPENING CLEANED SQUID TUBES
With a small, sharp knife, slit down one side of the tube and spread flat.

SCORING SQUID
Score inner side with parallel lines about ½ inch apart to make cross hatch pattern.

SKEWERING SQUID
Cut squid into 3-inch pieces. Thread strips across parallel skewers.

COOKS' NOTE
Squid needs to be cooked either very quickly over hight heat or very slowly over low heat, to avoid a tough, rubbery texture. When grilling, be sure to remove squid from the grill as soon as it is done.

SQUID WITH TOMATO AVOCADO SALSA

SERVES 4

FOR SALSA
4 tomatoes, seeded and diced
1 avocado, peeled, pitted, and diced
3 scallions, finely chopped
1 fresh green chile, seeded and
  finely chopped
1 tbsp finely chopped cilantro leaves
1 garlic clove, crushed

¼ cup fresh lime juice
3 tbsp olive oil

¾ lb large squid tubes, 10 inches long,
  cleaned (see page 68)
1 tbsp olive oil
salt, black pepper

ESSENTIAL EQUIPMENT
8 - 10-inch presoaked bamboo skewers

For salsa, combine tomatoes, avocado, scallion, chile, cilantro, garlic, lime juice, and oil. Add salt and pepper to taste.
Open and score squid tubes (see left). Toss in oil. Thread onto skewers as shown. Grill according to instructions below. Cut grilled squid into ½-inch strips. Combine squid strips with salsa. Add salt and pepper to taste. Serve hot or at room temperature.

OUTDOOR
Grill over medium-hot coals until just opaque, 2 minutes per side.

INDOOR
Preheat a ridged cast-iron grill pan over high heat. Cook until just opaque, 2 minutes per side.

THINK AHEAD
Make salsa up to 3 hours in advance. Cover tightly with plastic wrap and refrigerate.

SPICY MARINATED SQUID ON BRUSCHETTA

SERVES 4

¾ lb large squid tubes, 10 inches
  long, cleaned (see page 68)
1 tbsp olive oil
½ red onion, finely chopped
1 garlic clove, crushed
½ tsp crushed red pepper flakes
2 tbsp olive oil

1 tbsp fresh lemon juice
2 tomatoes, seeded and diced
1 tbsp chopped fresh mint leaves
salt, black pepper
8 - ½-inch-thick slices of day-old
  ciabatta or country-style bread

ESSENTIAL EQUIPMENT
8 - 10-inch presoaked bamboo skewers

Open and score squid tubes (see page 69). Toss squid in 1 tbsp olive oil and skewer
(see page 69). Grill squid according to instructions below. Cut grilled squid into
½-inch-wide strips. Combine onion, garlic, red pepper flakes, olive oil, lemon juice,
tomatoes, and mint in a bowl. Add squid and toss to coat evenly. Leave at room
temperature for 30 minutes. Toast bread until crisp and striped, 2 minutes per side.
Top with squid. Serve at room temperature or chilled.

OUTDOOR
Grill over medium-hot coals until just opaque,
1–2 minutes per side.

INDOOR
Preheat a ridged cast-iron grill pan over high heat.
Cook until just opaque, 1–2 minutes per side.

THINK AHEAD
Grill and marinate squid up to 1 day in advance. Cover and refrigerate.

LEMON CHARMOULA SQUID

SERVES 4

¾ lb large squid tubes, 10 inches
  long, cleaned (see page 68)
1 tbsp olive oil
1 recipe charmoula (see page 23)
1 lemon, peeled and chopped
  (see page 161)
salt, black pepper

ESSENTIAL EQUIPMENT
16 - 10-inch presoaked bamboo skewers

Open and score squid tubes (see page
69). Cut scored tubes in to 6 pieces. Toss
in olive oil. Thread onto parallel skewers
(see page 69), with 3 pieces per pair of
skewers. Grill according to instructions
below. Combine charmoula with lemon.
Toss squid with charmoula and lemon to
coat. Sprinkle with salt and pepper.
Serve hot, at room temperature, or chilled.

OUTDOOR
Grill over medium-hot
coals until just opaque,
2 minutes per side.

INDOOR
Preheat a ridged cast-
iron grill pan over high
heat. Cook until just
opaque, 2 minutes
per side.

THINK AHEAD
Grill squid and combine with charmoula and lemon
up to 1 day in advance. Cover and refrigerate.

COOKS' NOTE
For an authentic Moroccan flavor, use 1 finely
chopped preserved lemon in place of the fresh
lemon. Preserved lemons are available from Middle-
Eastern and gourmet stores (see page 167).

CUTTING A LOBSTER IN HALF
Place the lobster belly side down. Insert the tip of a large knife at the cross mark right behind the head and cut through the head (see above). Turn the lobster around. Holding it firmly by the head, cut it in half lengthwise from head to tail.

CHARGRILLED LOBSTER WITH GARLIC PARSLEY BUTTER

SERVES 4

4 large cooked lobsters
½ cup garlic parsley butter (see page 140), melted
lemon wedges

Cut lobster in half with a large sharp knife (see left). Scoop out the head sac and discard. Grill according to instructions below. Serve warm with lemon wedges and remaining butter drizzled over.

OUTDOOR
Grill shell side down over medium-hot coals, frequently brushing flesh with butter, until warmed through, 5 minutes.

INDOOR
Preheat broiler. Broil flesh side up, brushing with butter, until warmed through, 5 minutes.

THINK AHEAD
Split lobsters up to 2 hours in advance. Cover and refrigerate.

COOKS' NOTE
Cilantro chili butter (see page 140) in place of the garlic parsley butter, and lime wedges in place of lemon wedges make an excellent alternative recipe for this grilled lobster.

FLAME-ROASTED LOBSTER

SERVES 4

4 large cooked lobsters
1 recipe roasted garlic aïoli (see page 143)
lemon wedges

OUTDOOR
Grill whole lobster over medium coals until hot to the touch, 5 minutes per side. Bash open and serve warm with roasted garlic aïoli and lemon wedges.

MUSSELS IN BEER AND GARLIC

SERVES 4
4lb mussels
⅓ cup beer
2 garlic cloves, finely chopped
2 tbsp chopped flat-leaf parsley leaves
salt, black pepper

Scrub mussels under running water. Discard any that are broken or not tightly closed. To cook outdoors, fold 1 yard of foil in half for double thickness. Spread mussels over middle of foil. Scrunch up the edges of the foil and add the beer. Fold up edges to make a tray. To cook indoors, put mussels and beer in a large pan with a lid on. Grill or cook according to instructions below. Sprinkle with the garlic and parsley. Remove from heat when you can smell the garlic, 1 minute. Sprinkle with salt and pepper. Serve hot, discarding any mussels that have not opened.

OUTDOOR
Grill over medium-low coals until shells are open and the mussels turn opaque, 8–10 minutes. Open the foil but leave the edges up so no juices escape.

INDOOR
Steam over medium heat until shells are open and the mussels turn opaque, 6 minutes. Shake pan occasionally to ensure even cooking.

CLAMS IN CILANTRO CHILI BUTTER

SERVES 4
4lb clams
½ cup cilantro chili butter (see page 140), melted

Scrub clams under running water. Discard any that are broken or not tightly closed. To cook outdoors, fold 1 yard of foil in half for double thickness. Spread clams over middle of foil. Fold in the edges to make a tray. To cook indoors, put clams in a large dry pan and cover. Grill or cook according to instructions below. Add the melted butter and remove from the heat when butter is hot and fragrant, 1 minute. Serve hot, discarding any clams that have not opened.

OUTDOOR
Grill over medium-low coals until shells are open and the clams turn opaque, 8–10 minutes. Open the foil out but leave the edges raised so that no juices escape.

INDOOR
Cook over medium heat until shells open and the clams turn opaque, 6 minutes. Shake pan occasionally to ensure even cooking.

GOLDEN RULE FOR COOKING FISH

Never desert your post once fish is placed on the grill. Fish is naturally tender. Most fish requires only brief grilling to firm its flesh and to bring out its delicate flavor. Overcooked fish is dry and tasteless, and overcooking can happen in a matter of minutes.

SELECTING FISH FOR THE GRILL

• Oil rich fish with a firm meaty texture is the easiest to grill. This includes salmon, tuna, halibut, swordfish, snapper, and mackerel.
• Skin left on fish acts to protect the delicate flesh and turns deliciously crisp on the grill.
• Firm textured flesh also means that the fish will hold together better.

GETTING IT READY

• Cut deep slashes through the skin side of fish fillets and through to the bone of whole fish to allow flavor, smoke, and heat to penetrate evenly.
• Liberal oiling is important for all types of fish to prevent it from drying out, except in the case of very oily skinned fish, like sardines.

MARINATING

• Fish requires only a very brief amount of time in a marinade. Tender fish flesh absorbs a marinade faster than the denser flesh of red meat. When left in an acidic marinade for too long, fish flesh will literally start to cook and turn white.
• Marinate fish for no longer than 2 hours in the refrigerator. It is better to drizzle or brush an oil rich flavor mix over the fish flesh than to give it a long soak in a wet acidic marinade.

PUTTING IT ON

• Before putting fish on the grill make sure to bring it to room temperature. Remove it from the refrigerator no more than 30 minutes beforehand. This will ensure that it cooks evenly and quickly.
• Use a hinged grill rack to turn fish that is tender and delicate. It will help keep whole fish intact and prevent fillets from breaking apart.
• When turning fish with a metal spatula, turn only once to avoid the tendency of fish to fall apart.

TAKING IT OFF

Fish will continue cooking a significant amount after it is removed from the grill. To avoid overcooked, dry, and flavorless fish, remove as soon as it is done. You can always put it back on but once it is overcooked there is no quick fix. Fish is done when it is opaque through to the center but still moist and tender. Cook fish until the internal temperature reads 140°F.

FINAL FLAVORING

• Salting raw fish draws out moisture and toughens the flesh. Always add seasoning after cooking but be sure not to forget.

• Add complementary flavors and moisture after removing it from the grill, with sauces, salsas, and dressings (consult pages 130–143 for more ideas).

CHARGRILLED SWORDFISH WITH ROASTED PEPPER AND BASIL SALSA

SERVES 4

4 - 6oz swordfish steaks
1 tbsp olive oil
salt, black pepper

1 recipe roasted pepper and basil salsa (see page 138)

ESSENTIAL EQUIPMENT
hinged wire rack, or alternatively a long metal spatula for turning fish on the grill

Brush the steaks with olive oil on both sides. Grill according to instructions below. Sprinkle with salt and pepper. Serve hot with salsa.

OUTDOOR
Grill over medium-hot coals until just opaque, 3 minutes per side.

INDOOR
Preheat a ridged cast-iron grill pan over high heat. Cook until just opaque, 3 minutes per side.

COOKS' NOTE
Salsa fresca (see page 133), cilantro coconut sauce (see page 138), salsa verde (see page 134), and chili lime mayonnaise (see page 143) all complement swordfish wonderfully. Shark, salmon, halibut, or monkfish make excellent alternatives to grilling swordfish with this simple, no-frills method.

SPICE-CRUSTED TUNA WITH THAI CITRUS DRESSING

SERVES 4

4 - ½lb tuna fillets,
  1 inch thick
1 tbsp peanut oil
2 tbsp coriander seeds
2 tbsp black peppercorns
lime wedges

FOR DRESSING
2 lemon grass stalks
1 fresh red chile, seeded and finely
  sliced
1 tbsp finely chopped cilantro leaves
2 tbsp fish sauce
2 tbsp peanut oil
⅓ cup fresh lime juice

ESSENTIAL EQUIPMENT
hinged wire rack, or alternatively a long metal spatula for turning fish on the grill

For dressing, remove and discard the tough outer skin from the lemon grass stalks
and finely slice. Combine lemon grass, chile, cilantro, fish sauce, oil, and lime juice.
Brush fillets on both sides with oil. Crush the coriander seeds and peppercorns
(see page 161). Press crushed seeds onto both sides of fillets. Grill according to
instructions below. Pour dressing over the top and serve hot or at room temperature
with lime wedges.

OUTDOOR
Grill over hot coals, 2 minutes per side for rare, 3
minutes per side for medium rare, 4 minutes per
side for well done.

INDOOR
Preheat a ridged cast-iron grill pan over high heat.
Cook for 2 minutes per side for rare, 3 minutes per
side for medium rare, 4 minutes per side for well done.

THINK AHEAD
Coat tuna with spices up to 4 hours in advance. Cover and refrigerate. Make dressing up to 3 hours in
advance. Cover and refrigerate.

COOKS' NOTE
Salsa fresca (see page 133), creamy avocado salsa (see page 132), roasted pepper and basil salsa (see page
138), or avocado mango salsa (see page 136) are all delicious served with this simple tuna recipe.

CHARGRILLED SARDINES

SERVES 4

24 - 1oz ungutted small
  sardines
salt, black pepper

ESSENTIAL EQUIPMENT
hinged wire rack

Grill sardines according to instructions
below. Sprinkle with salt and pepper.
Serve hot with lemon wedges.

OUTDOOR
Place sardines in hinged
wire rack. Grill over
medium-hot coals until
opaque throughout and
crispy on the outside,
3 minutes per side.

INDOOR
Don't even attempt to
broil sardines indoors,
unless you are planning
to move. The aroma will
linger forever!

COOKS' NOTE
If you grill large sardines they will need cleaning
and gutting. Allow 3 sardines per person. Grill for
5 minutes per side.

GRILL-ROASTED SEA BASS WITH FENNEL, LEMON, AND OLIVE OIL

SERVES 4

4 - 6oz unskinned sea bass
  fillets
1 fennel bulb, grated
4 garlic cloves, finely sliced
2 tbsp chopped flat-leaf parsley leaves
1½ tsp salt
1 tsp black pepper
1 tsp fennel seeds
1 tbsp olive oil
1 lemon, sliced
1 recipe salsa verde (see page 134),
  optional

ESSENTIAL EQUIPMENT
4 - 16-inch squares heavy duty foil

Cut several shallow diagonal slashes about 1 inch apart on the skin side of each fillet. Divide the fennel, garlic, and parsley among the foil squares, spreading in an even layer on one half of each foil piece. Place the fish skin side up on top. Sprinkle with salt, pepper, and fennel seeds. Drizzle with oil. Place lemon slices on top. Fold the other half of the foil over the top of the fish. Fold over edges to seal foil packets tightly. Grill or bake according to instructions below. Serve hot in foil packet with salsa verde.

OUTDOOR
Grill over medium-hot coals until fish is opaque throughout, 8–10 minutes. Flip foil packet over half way through grilling.

INDOOR
Preheat oven to 400°F. Bake until fish is opaque throughout, 8–10 minutes

THINK AHEAD
Prepare foil packets up to 2 hours in advance. Refrigerate.

COOKS' NOTE
Sea bream, mullet, grouper, or red snapper fillets make good alternatives to sea bass in this fennel-fragrant recipe.

HERBED SALMON WITH TOMATO VINAIGRETTE

SERVES 4

2 - ¾lb tail-end salmon fillets
juice of 1 lemon
2 tbsp finely chopped fresh dill
2 tsp salt
1 tsp black pepper
½ tsp coriander seeds, crushed
  (see page 161)

FOR VINAIGRETTE
1 garlic clove, crushed
1 shallot, finely chopped
2 tbsp red wine vinegar
¼ cup (60ml) olive oil
3 tomatoes, seeded and diced
salt, black pepper

ESSENTIAL EQUIPMENT
hinged grill rack

For vinaigrette, combine garlic, shallot, and vinegar. Let stand for 30 minutes. Whisk in the oil and tomatoes. Add salt and pepper to taste. Place salmon fillets skin side down. Drizzle lemon juice evenly over both fillets. Sprinkle 1 salmon fillet with dill, salt, pepper, and coriander seeds. Place uncoated fillet skin side up over the other fillet. Grill according to instructions below. Cut into four portions. Top with vinaigrette and serve hot.

OUTDOOR
Place sandwiched fillets in hinged grill rack. Grill over medium-hot coals until skin is very crisp and flesh has just turned opaque but is still moist and pink in the center, 5 minutes per side.

INDOOR
Preheat oven to 400°F. Place sandwiched fillets on rack in roasting tin. Roast until flesh has just turned opaque but is still moist and pink in the center, 15–20 minutes.

THINK AHEAD
Sandwich fillets together up to 2 hours in advance. Cover tightly with plastic wrap and refrigerate. Make vinaigrette up to 6 hours in advance. Cover and refrigerate.

MOROCCAN SPICED MACKEREL

SERVES 4

4 - 1lb whole mackerel
1 recipe charmoula (see page 23)
salt, black pepper

ESSENTIAL EQUIPMENT
hinged wire rack, or alternatively a long metal spatula for turning fish on the grill

Cut slashes about 2 inches apart down both sides of each fish, cutting through to the bones. Spread ½ tbsp of the charmoula down both sides of the inside cavity of each fish. Grill according to instructions below. Sprinkle with salt and pepper. Serve hot with the remaining charmoula.

OUTDOOR
Grill over medium-hot coals until flesh is opaque at the bone and skin is very crispy, 5 minutes per side.

INDOOR
Preheat broiler. Broil until the flesh is opaque at the bone and the skin is very crispy, 5 minutes per side.

THINK AHEAD
Prepare mackerel for grilling up to 2 hours in advance. Cover tightly with plastic wrap and refrigerate.

COOKS' NOTE
Chimi churri sauce (see page 135) used as an alternative to the charmoula is also very good for flavoring mackerel.

WASABI SOY SALMON WITH SESAME SOBA NOODLES

SERVES 4

4 - 6oz salmon fillets
1 tsp wasabi paste
2 tsp brown sugar
1 tbsp sake

1 tbsp fresh lime juice
3 tbsp shoyu (Japanese soy sauce)
1 recipe sesame soba noodle salad
(see page 148)

ESSENTIAL EQUIPMENT
hinged wire rack, or alternatively a long metal spatula for turning fish on the grill

Combine wasabi, sugar, sake, lime, and shoyu. Set aside 2 tbsp for drizzling. Brush the fillets on both sides with the remaining mixture. Grill according to instructions below. Serve hot with sesame soba noodle salad and drizzle with reserved mixture.

OUTDOOR
Grill over medium-hot coals until the flesh just turns opaque but is still moist and pink in the middle, 3–4 minutes per side.

INDOOR
Preheat a ridged cast-iron grill pan over high heat. Cook until the flesh just turns opaque but is still moist and pink in the middle, 3–4 minutes per side.

THINK AHEAD
Brush the salmon up to 30 minutes in advance.

CHARGRILLED TROUT WITH GARLIC PARSLEY BUTTER

SERVES 4
4 - ½ lb trout without head, butterflied (see left)
1 tbsp peanut oil
salt, black pepper
lemon wedges
4 - ½-inch slices garlic parsley butter (see page 140)

ESSENTIAL EQUIPMENT
hinged wire rack, or alternatively a long metal spatula for turning fish on the grill

Brush flesh side of trout with oil. Place trout in hinged wire rack, if using. Grill according to instructions below. Sprinkle with salt and pepper. Serve hot with garlic parsley butter and lemon wedges.

OUTDOOR
Grill skin side down over medium-hot coals until skin starts to turn crisp, 2 minutes. Turn and grill for 1 minute. Turn again. Grill until flesh just turns opaque, is firm, and the skin is crispy, another 2 minutes.

INDOOR
Preheat broiler. Broil skin side up until skin starts to turn crispy, 2 minutes. Turn and broil for 1 minute. Turn again. Broil until flesh just turns opaque, is firm, and the skin is crispy, another 2 minutes.

THINK AHEAD
Butterfly trout up to 8 hours in advance. Cover tightly with plastic wrap and refrigerate.

BUTTERFLYING TROUT
Lay a gutted, headless trout skin side down on a cutting board. Working down one side, slide the tip of a sharp knife between the rib bones and flesh. Use small stroking cuts to release the bones. Repeat on the opposite side.

Place fish skin side down and open flat. Lift up backbone from head to tail and cut off with scissors.

CHARGRILLED TROUT WITH GARLIC PARSLEY BUTTER

RED SNAPPER TACOS WITH CHILI LIME MAYO

SERVES 4

4 - 6oz unskinned red
  snapper fillets
1 garlic clove, crushed
½ tsp ground cumin
½ tsp chili powder
½ tsp dried oregano
1 tbsp fresh lime juice
2 tbsp olive oil
salt, black pepper
4 8-inch flour tortillas or fresh
  corn tortillas
1 avocado, peeled, pitted, and diced
2 tbsp cilantro leaves
1 tbsp finely diced red chili
1 recipe chili lime mayonnaise
  (see page 143)

ESSENTIAL EQUIPMENT
*hinged wire rack, or alternatively a long metal
spatula for turning fish on the grill*

Combine the garlic, cumin, chili powder,
oregano, lime juice, and oil. Brush
mixture over fillets. Place fillets in
hinged wire rack, if using. Grill fillets
according to instructions below. Sprinkle
with salt and pepper. Warm tortillas
directly over the grill or in the hot grill
pan for 30 seconds each side. Cut fish
into 1½-inch cubes. Divide among
warmed tortillas. Top with avocado dice,
cilantro leaves, red chili, and chili lime
mayonnaise. Fold in half and serve hot.

OUTDOOR
Grill fillets over
medium-hot coals,
skin-side down for
3 minutes. Turn and grill
until opaque throughout,
another 3 minutes.

INDOOR
Preheat a ridged cast-
iron grill pan. Cook
fillets skin-side down for
3 minutes. Turn and
cook until opaque
throughout, another
3 minutes.

THINK AHEAD
Brush the snapper with seasoning up to 30 minutes
in advance.

COOKS' NOTE
Grouper or sea bass fillets are excellent alternatives
to red snapper.

ALTERNATIVE SEAFOOD FOR PROVENÇAL GRILLADE

Feel free to make any of the following substitutions:

6 small, cooked, soft shell crabs in place of dungeness crab.

2 - 6oz fillets grouper or bass, in place of red snapper and striped mullet fillets.

2 - 6oz salmon or swordfish steaks, in place of tuna.

12 jumbo head-on shrimp, in place of lobster tails.

8 skewered scallops, grilled until just opaque, 2 minutes per side, as an optional addition.

PROVENÇAL SEAFOOD GRILLADE WITH LEMON FENNEL DRESSING AND ROASTED GARLIC AÏOLI

SERVES 4–6

2 garlic cloves, crushed
2 tbsp pernod
2 tbsp olive oil
4 large cooked dungeness crab
1lb tuna fillet, 1 inch thick
2 - 6oz red snapper fillets
2 - 6oz striped mullet fillets
8 cooked lobster tails

FOR DRESSING
⅓ cup olive oil
2 tbsp fresh lemon juice
2 tbsp red wine vinegar
1 tbsp finely chopped fresh
  fennel tops or dill
salt, black pepper

1 recipe roasted garlic aïoli
  (see page 143)
crusty bread and lemon wedges

ESSENTIAL EQUIPMENT
long metal spatula

For dressing, whisk oil into lemon and vinegar. Stir in fennel or dill. Add salt and pepper to taste. Combine garlic, pernod, and oil. Using a hammer or rolling pin, crack crab claws just enough to expose the interior to seasoning. Brush all the seafood with the garlic mixture. Grill according to instructions below. Cut cooked tuna and fish fillets into chunks. Arrange seafood on platter. Drizzle with dressing. Serve hot or at room temperature with roasted garlic aïoli, crusty bread, and lemon wedges.

OUTDOOR
Grill seafood over medium-hot coals, using spatula to turn. Grill tuna for 3 minutes per side for rare, 4 minutes per side for medium rare, 5 minutes per side for well done. Grill fish fillets, skin side down first, until opaque throughout, 3 minutes per side. Grill shellfish until warmed through, 3 minutes per side.

INDOOR
This recipe is inappropriate for indoor cooking.

THINK AHEAD
Crack and brush seafood up to 2 hours in advance. Cover with plastic wrap and refrigerate.

GETTING IT READY

Chicken should be grilled in pieces of uniform shape and thickness. This is essential to ensure safe, even cooking and to guarantee the best results.

• Boning chicken (see page 104), splitting and flattening whole birds (see page 110), and butterflying boneless breasts (see page 94) allow chicken to cook evenly and prevent overcooked white meat.
• Slashing (see page 102) and making shallow cuts (see page 92) open the greatest surface area to flavor, smoke and heat. This allows marinades to penetrate more deeply and chicken to cook more quickly.

MARINATING

The intense heat of an outdoor grill can dry out naturally lean chicken meat, especially when it has been boned and skinned. Marinating is an essential step to retaining moisture during cooking, but it is also important not to overdo it. Overmarinating will draw moisture out from, toughen, and when acid is present, literally begin to cook the meat. The result is poultry that looks grayish white and rubbery. Marinate for the recommended time only.

PUTTING IT ON

Before putting chicken on the grill make sure to bring it to room temperature, by removing it from the refrigerator no more than 20 minutes beforehand. This will ensure that it cooks evenly and quickly.

• Be sure to brush poultry liberally with oil to keep it moist during grilling.
• Cooking chicken for a crowd? Get ahead by precooking on the bone chicken pieces (such as wings, drums, and whole split birds) in a preheated 400°F oven for 15 minutes. Transfer to the grill when your guests arrive and reduce the required cooking time by approximately 10 minutes.

TAKING IT OFF

Check doneness by making a cut into the meat with a small, sharp knife (see page 13), before removing chicken from the grill. It is always better to check doneness at the grill than to discover undercooked meat on the plate. Chicken is done when it is opaque throughout with no trace of pink at the bone. Watch boneless cuts carefully to avoid overcooking and to ensure maximum juiciness and succulence.

FINAL FLAVORING

We add salt just before serving because salting any sooner will draw out the chicken's flavorful juices. But don't forget to season before putting food on the table.

SAFETY TIPS FOR CHICKEN

The raw juices of uncooked chicken contain bacteria that can easily contaminate the cooked meat and other foods you are preparing. For healthy eating, be sure to take the following precautions:

• Always wash hands with soap and hot water before and after handling uncooked chicken.

• Never leave uncooked chicken at room temperature for more than 20 minutes.

• Never reuse a chicken marinade or baste cooked chicken with a marinade after it has been used.

• Never put cooked chicken back into the unwashed container in which it was marinating.

SLASHING CHICKEN BREASTS
With a sharp knife, cut 3 parallel slashes through skin, about ¼ inch deep.

COOKS' NOTE
We slash the chicken breasts to allow the flavors of the seasonings and marinades to penetrate the chicken more fully.

CITRUS RECADO CHICKEN BREASTS

SERVES 4

2 garlic cloves, crushed	2 tbsp canola oil
1 tsp chili powder	2 tbsp fresh lime juice
½ tsp dried oregano	¼ cup orange juice
½ tsp dried thyme	4 boneless chicken breast halves,
½ tsp ground cumin	slashed (see left)
½ tsp ground coriander	salt
½ tsp black pepper	1 recipe avocado mango salsa
¼ tsp ground cinnamon	(see page 136), optional
1 tbsp dark brown sugar	

Combine garlic, chili powder, oregano, thyme, cumin, coriander, pepper, cinnamon, sugar, oil, lime juice, and orange juice. Add chicken and toss to coat evenly. Cover and refrigerate for 30 minutes, turning once. Grill according to instructions below. Sprinkle with salt. Serve hot with avocado mango salsa, optional.

OUTDOOR
Grill skin side down over medium-hot coals until skin is crisp, 7 minutes. Turn and continue grilling until chicken is opaque with no trace of pink, another 5 minutes.

INDOOR
Preheat broiler. Broil skin side up until skin is crisp, 7 minutes. Turn and continue cooking until chicken is opaque with no trace of pink, another 5 minutes.

THINK AHEAD
Marinate chicken up to 2 hours in advance. Cover and refrigerate, turning several times in marinade.

COOKS' NOTE
We prefer the mildly spicy sweet heat of ancho chili powder in this Mexican-style dish. These wrinkled reddish brown chiles are actually dried poblanos. They are widely used in Mexican cooking. For complete authenticity, also try to find dried Mexican oregano. Both are available from specialty shops or gourmet mail order sources (see page 167).

HERBED BALSAMIC CHICKEN BREASTS

SERVES 4

2 garlic cloves, crushed
1 tsp herbes de provence
½ tsp black pepper
1 tbsp Dijon mustard
1 tbsp olive oil
¼ cup balsamic vinegar
salt, black pepper
4 boneless chicken breast halves, slashed (see page 92)
1 recipe roasted red pepper aïoli (see page 143), optional

Combine garlic, herbes de provence, pepper, mustard, oil, and vinegar. Add chicken and toss to coat evenly. Cover and refrigerate for 30 minutes, turning once. Grill according to instructions below. Sprinkle with salt and pepper. Serve hot with roasted red pepper aïoli, optional.

OUTDOOR
Grill skin side down on medium-hot coals until crisp, 7 minutes. Turn and continue grilling until chicken is opaque with no trace of pink, another 5 minutes.

INDOOR
Preheat broiler. Broil skin side up until skin is crisp, about 7 minutes. Turn and continue cooking until chicken is opaque with no trace of pink, another 5 minutes.

THINK AHEAD
Marinate chicken breasts up to 2 hours in advance. Cover and refrigerate, turning every 15–20 minutes.

COOKS' NOTE
Herbes de Provence, a fragrant dry herb mix that includes fennel, lavender, and summer savory, is a kitchen cupboard essential. Sprinkle over poultry, meats, fish, or vegetables to bring the scent and flavor of sun-soaked Provence into your kitchen.

GINGER SOY CHICKEN BREASTS

SERVES 4

2 tbsp grated fresh ginger
3 garlic cloves, crushed
2 tbsp dark brown sugar
2 tsp sesame seeds
2 tsp toasted sesame oil
1 tbsp medium dry sherry
½ cup soy sauce
4 boneless chicken breast halves, slashed (see page 92)
salt, black pepper
1 recipe cilantro coconut sauce (see page 138), optional

Combine ginger, garlic, sugar, sesame seeds, sesame oil, sherry, and soy sauce. Add chicken and toss to coat evenly. Cover and refrigerate for 30 minutes, turning once. Grill according to instructions below. Sprinkle with salt and pepper. Serve hot with cilantro coconut sauce, optional.

OUTDOOR
Grill skin side down on medium-hot coals until crisp, 7 minutes. Turn and continue grilling until chicken is opaque with no trace of pink, another 5 minutes.

INDOOR
Preheat broiler. Broil skin side up until skin is crisp, 7 minutes. Turn and continue cooking until chicken is opaque with no trace of pink, another 5 minutes.

THINK AHEAD
Marinate chicken breasts up to 2 hours in advance. Cover and refrigerate, turning every 15–20 minutes.

BUTTERFLYING CHICKEN BREAST HALF

With one hand on the breast half to hold it in place, slice through the middle horizontally to cut almost in half. Open out flat.

THINK AHEAD
Butterfly breast half up to 1 day in advance. Cover tightly with plastic wrap and refrigerate.

COOKS' NOTE
Butterflying makes chicken breast halves into thin fillets that can be cooked in a flash. It also produces the perfect pocket for stuffing.

THAI LIME AND COCONUT CHICKEN

SERVES 4

2 lemon grass stalks
3 fresh green chiles, seeded and chopped
2 garlic cloves, chopped
3 scallions, chopped
1 handful cilantro leaves
½ tsp ground cumin
½ tsp ground white pepper
½ tsp turmeric
1 tsp ground coriander

grated zest 1 lime
3 tbsp fresh lime juice
2 tsp grated fresh ginger
1 tbsp fish sauce
½ cup coconut milk
4 boneless, skinless chicken breast halves, butterflied (see left)
salt, black pepper
1 recipe fresh papaya sambal (see page 137), optional

Remove and discard the tough outer skin from the lemon grass stalks and roughly chop. Put lemon grass, chiles, garlic, scallion, cilantro, cumin, pepper, turmeric, ground coriander, lime zest, lime juice, ginger, fish sauce, and coconut milk in food processor or blender; pulse until smooth. In a bowl, toss chicken with lemon grass mixture. Cover and refrigerate for 1 hour. Grill according to instructions below. Sprinkle with salt and pepper. Serve hot with fresh papaya sambal, optional.

OUTDOOR
Grill over medium hot coals until the chicken is opaque, with no trace of pink, 3 minutes per side.

INDOOR
Preheat broiler. Broil until the chicken is opaque with no trace of pink, 3 minutes per side.

THINK AHEAD
Make marinade up to 3 days in advance. Cover and refrigerate. Marinate chicken up to 4 hours in advance. Cover and refrigerate.

LEMON OREGANO CHICKEN BAGUETTE

SERVES 4

4 boneless, skinless chicken breast
  halves, butterflied (see page 94)
1 lemon, peeled and chopped
  (see page 161)
2 garlic cloves, crushed
2 tsp dried oregano
2 tbsp olive oil

1 tsp black pepper
1 baguette
salt
1 beefsteak tomato, sliced
1 handful crisp salad leaves
1 recipe roasted garlic aïoli
  (see page 143)

Toss chicken breast halves with lemon, garlic, oregano, oil, and pepper. Cover and
refrigerate for 20 minutes. Cut baguette into 4 equal-sized pieces. Split and toast
baguette on the cut side until just crisp, 1 minute. Grill chicken according to
instructions below. Sprinkle with salt. Fill baguette with tomatoes, salad, chicken,
and aïoli. Serve warm.

OUTDOOR
Grill over medium hot coals until chicken is opaque,
with no trace of pink, 3 minutes per side.

INDOOR
Preheat broiler. Broil until the chicken is opaque
with no trace of pink, 3 minutes per side.

THINK AHEAD
Marinate chicken up to 2 hours in advance. Cover and refrigerate, turning in the marinade every
15–20 minutes.

SKEWERED BAJAAN CHICKEN

SERVES 4

2 garlic cloves
4 scallions
½ red onion
½ scotch bonnet chile, seeded or
  1 fresh red chile, seeded
1 handful flat-leaf parsley leaves
1 tsp fresh thyme leaves
2 tbsp fresh lime juice

2 tbsp canola oil
¼ tsp ground allspice
salt, black pepper
4 boneless chicken breast halves,
  butterflied (see page 94)
1 recipe creamy avocado salsa
  (see page 132), optional

ESSENTIAL EQUIPMENT
4 - 10-inch presoaked bamboo skewers

Place garlic, scallions, red onion, chile, parsley, thyme, lime juice, oil, and allspice in
a food processor or blender; pulse to a paste. Add salt and pepper to taste. Open out
chicken breast halves and spread 1 tbsp paste on each opened breast. Fold breasts
over again. Thread a skewer through cut edges of breast, weaving in and out several
times to hold the chicken edges together. Grill according to instructions below.
Sprinkle with salt and pepper. Serve hot with creamy avocado salsa, optional.

OUTDOOR
Grill skin side down over medium-hot coals until skin
is crisp, 7 minutes. Turn and continue grilling until
chicken is opaque with no trace of pink, another
5 minutes.

INDOOR
Preheat broiler. Broil skin side up until skin is crisp,
7 minutes. Turn and continue cooking until chicken
is opaque with no trace of pink, another 5 minutes.

THINK AHEAD
Stuff breasts up to 1 day in advance. Wrap in plastic wrap and refrigerate.

COOKS' NOTE
Butterflying breast produces a perfect pocket for stuffing. As an alternative to bajaan stuffing, substitute
charmoula (see page 23), spicy jerk rub (see page 24), or the simple combination of crushed garlic and
chopped fresh herbs.

CHICKEN, PROSCIUTTO, AND SAGE SKEWERS

SERVES 4

4 boneless, skinless chicken
  breast halves
1 garlic clove, crushed
1 tsp black pepper
2 tbsp fresh lemon juice
3 tbsp olive oil
6 slices prosciutto, cut in half
12 fresh sage leaves
4 - 1-inch cubes country style
  day-old bread
1 recipe roasted red pepper aïoli
  (see page 143)

ESSENTIAL EQUIPMENT
4 - 14-inch flat metal skewers

Cut each breast lengthwise into 3 strips.
Combine garlic, pepper, lemon, and
2 tbsp oil. Add chicken strips and toss
to coat evenly. Place one sage leaf on top
of each prosciutto half slice. Place one
chicken strip on top of the sage. Roll up
prosciutto and sage around each chicken
strip. Thread 3 wrapped strips lengthwise
onto each skewer. Toss bread cubes in
1 tbsp olive oil. Thread 1 bread cube
onto the end of each skewer. Grill
according to instructions below. Serve
hot with roasted red pepper aïoli.

OUTDOOR
Grill over medium-hot
coals, turning every
2 minutes, until cooked
through, 8–10 minutes.

INDOOR
Preheat broiler. Broil,
turning every 2 minutes,
until cooked through,
8–10 minutes.

THINK AHEAD
Skewer chicken but not bread up to 6 hours in
advance. Cover and refrigerate. Toss and skewer
bread cubes just before grilling.

LEMON YOGURT CHICKEN WRAP

SERVES 4

4 boneless, skinless chicken
  breast halves
2 garlic cloves, crushed
¼ tsp ground cinnamon
¼ tsp ground allspice
1 tsp black pepper
1 tbsp olive oil
3 tbsp fresh lemon juice
2 tbsp Greek-style yogurt

4 pita or flatbreads
1 handful shredded iceberg
  or romaine lettuce
4 tomatoes, sliced
8 radishes, sliced
salt
1 recipe roasted garlic aïoli (see
  page 143)

ESSENTIAL EQUIPMENT
4 - 14-inch flat metal skewers

Cut each breast half lengthwise into 3 strips. Combine garlic, cinnamon, allspice, pepper, oil, lemon juice, and yogurt. Add chicken strips and toss to coat evenly. Cover and refrigerate for 30 minutes. Thread 3 chicken strips lengthwise on each skewer. Grill according to instructions below. Split open and separate each warmed pita into 2 halves. Stack 2 pita halves cut side up. Using a fork, slide the chicken pieces from 1 skewer onto the pita. Top with a quarter of the lettuce, tomatoes, and radishes. Top with aïoli. Add salt and pepper and roll up. Repeat with remaining pita, chicken, lettuce, tomatoes, radishes, and aïoli. Serve hot.

OUTDOOR
Grill over medium-hot coals, turning every 2 minutes, until cooked through, 8–10 minutes. Place pita halves directly on the grill until just warm, about 30 seconds per side.

INDOOR
Preheat broiler. Broil, turning every 2 minutes, until cooked through, 8–10 minutes. Place pita halves briefly under broiler until warm, 15 seconds per side.

THINK AHEAD
Marinate chicken up to 3 hours in advance. Cover and refrigerate.

SWEET CHILI CHICKEN

SERVES 4

4 boneless, skinless chicken
  breast halves
1 fresh red chile, seeded and
  finely chopped
2 garlic cloves, crushed
1 tbsp grated fresh ginger
¼ cup honey
2 tbsp soy sauce
¼ cup fresh lime juice

FOR GARNISHES

1 scallion, diagonally sliced
1 fresh red chile, seeded and
  finely sliced
1 tbsp fresh mint leaves
1 tbsp cilantro leaves

ESSENTIAL EQUIPMENT
4 - 14-inch flat metal skewers

Cut each breast half lengthwise into 3 strips. Combine chile, garlic, ginger, honey, soy sauce, and lime juice. Reserve ¼ cup mixture. Add chicken to remaining mixture and toss to coat evenly. Cover and refrigerate for 30 minutes. Thread 3 chicken strips lengthwise on each skewer. Grill according to instructions below. Drizzle reserved sweet chili mixture over top. Sprinkle with scallion, chili, mint, and cilantro. Serve hot.

OUTDOOR
Grill over medium-hot coals, turning every 2 minutes, until cooked through, 8–10 minutes.

INDOOR
Preheat broiler. Broil, turning every 2 minutes, until cooked through, 8–10 minutes.

THINK AHEAD
Marinate chicken up to 2 hours in advance. Cover and refrigerate.

COOKS' NOTE
This is Asian finger food. We also like to wrap up each succulent piece of chicken with its fragrant and spicy garnishes in a crisp, cool lettuce cup.

CUTTING OFF WING TIPS
To remove the wing tip, use a sharp pair of kitchen scissors and cut at the joint.

THREADING CHICKEN WINGS ONTO SKEWERS
Make sure that the skewers pass through the middle to secure both joints.

THAI SPICED CHICKEN WINGS

MAKES 20

2 lemon grass stalks
2 tbsp grated fresh ginger
5 garlic cloves, crushed
1 red onion, quartered
grated zest of 1 lime
2 tsp crushed red pepper flakes
¹/₂ tsp ground coriander
¹/₂ tsp ground cumin

½ tsp paprika
2 tsp salt
1 tbsp peanut oil
6 tbsp dark brown sugar
6 tbsp tomato paste
20 large chicken wings, tips removed (see left)

ESSENTIAL EQUIPMENT
8 - 14-inch flat metal skewers

Remove and discard the tough outer skin from the lemon grass stalks and roughly chop. Place lemon grass, ginger, garlic, onion, lime zest, red pepper flakes, coriander, cumin, paprika, salt, oil, sugar, and tomato paste in a food processor or blender; pulse until smooth. In a bowl, combine the mixture with the wings and toss to coat evenly. Cover and refrigerate for 2 hours. Thread the wings onto parallel skewers (see left). Grill according to instructions below. Serve hot.

OUTDOOR
Grill the wings over medium-hot coals for 15–20 minutes, turning every 5 minutes, until the meat at the bone is opaque.

INDOOR
Preheat broiler. Arrange the wings on a wire rack over a broiler rack. Broil for 15–20 minutes, turning once, until the meat at the bone is opaque.

THINK AHEAD
Marinate the wings up to 8 hours in advance. Make marinade up to 1 week in advance. Cover and refrigerate.

HONEY SOY CHICKEN WINGS

MAKES 20

6 tbsp dark soy sauce
3 tbsp dry sherry
2 tbsp honey
20 large chicken wings, tips removed (see page 100)
1 recipe spicy peanut sauce (see page 136), optional

ESSENTIAL EQUIPMENT
8 - 14-inch flat metal skewers

Combine soy sauce, sherry, and honey in a bowl. Add the wings and toss to coat evenly. Cover and refrigerate for 2 hours. Thread the wings onto parallel skewers (see page 100). Grill according to instructions below. Serve hot with spicy peanut sauce, optional.

OUTDOOR
Grill over medium-hot coals for 15–20 minutes, turning every 5 minutes, until the meat at the bone is opaque.

INDOOR
Preheat broiler. Arrange the wings on a wire rack over a broiler rack. Grill for 15–20 minutes, turning once, until the meat at the bone is opaque.

THINK AHEAD
Marinate the wings up to 8 hours in advance. Cover and refrigerate.

SPICY LIME CHICKEN WINGS

MAKES 20

2 limes, peeled and chopped (see page 161)
2 garlic cloves, crushed
1 tsp chili powder
1 tsp paprika
2 tsp sugar
20 large chicken wings, tips (see page 100)
2 tsp salt
1 recipe creamy avocado salsa (see page 132), optional

ESSENTIAL EQUIPMENT
8 - 14-inch flat metal skewers

Combine lime flesh, garlic, chili powder, paprika, and sugar in a bowl. Add the wings and toss to coat evenly. Cover and refrigerate for 2 hours. Thread the wings onto parallel skewers (see page 100). Sprinkle evenly with salt. Grill according to instructions below. Serve hot with creamy avocado salsa for dipping, optional.

OUTDOOR
Grill wings over medium-hot coals for 15–20 minutes, turning every 5 minutes, until the meat at the bone is opaque.

INDOOR
Preheat broiler. Arrange the wings on a wire rack over a broiler rack. Grill for 15–20 minutes, turning once, until the meat at the bone is opaque.

THINK AHEAD
Marinate the wings up to 8 hours in advance. Cover and refrigerate.

SLASHING DRUMSTICKS

With sharp kitchen scissors, snip through skin to make deep cuts to the bone on both sides of the drumstick.

COOKS' NOTE

We slash drumsticks not only to allow flavoring to penetrate deeply, but to ensure that the meat is cooked through to the bone as quickly and evenly as possible.

HONEY MUSTARD CHICKEN DRUMSTICKS

SERVES 4

6 garlic cloves, crushed
3 tbsp honey
2 tbsp Dijon mustard
2 tbsp soy sauce
1 tbsp fresh lemon juice

1 tsp black pepper
8 drumsticks, slashed (see left)
salt
1 recipe roasted garlic aïoli (see page 143), optional

Combine garlic, honey, mustard, soy sauce, lemon juice, and pepper. Add drumsticks and toss to coat evenly. Cover and refrigerate for 1 hour. Grill according to instructions below. Sprinkle with salt. Serve hot with roasted garlic aïoli for dipping, optional.

OUTDOOR

Grill over medium hot coals , turning every 3 minutes, until the chicken is opaque with no trace of pink at the bone, 15 minutes.

INDOOR

Preheat overhead broiler. Broil, turning every 3 minutes, until the chicken is opaque with no trace of pink at the bone, 15 minutes.

THINK AHEAD

Marinate drumsticks up to 6 hours in advance. Cover and refrigerate.

SPICY TANDOORI CHICKEN DRUMSTICKS

SERVES 4

juice of 1 lemon
2 tsp black pepper
8 chicken drumsticks, slashed
  (see page 102)
2 garlic cloves, crushed
1 tbsp grated fresh ginger
3 tbsp spicy tandoori mix
  (see page 25)
⅔ cup Greek-style yogurt
salt

Toss drumsticks with lemon juice and pepper. Cover and refrigerate for 30 minutes. Drain lemon juice. Add garlic, ginger, tandoori mix, sour cream, and yogurt to drumsticks. Toss to coat evenly. Cover and refrigerate for 1 hour. Shake off excess marinade and grill according to instructions below. Serve hot.

OUTDOOR
Grill over medium hot coals, turning every 3 minutes, until opaque with no trace of pink at the bone, 15 minutes.

INDOOR
Preheat broiler. Broil, turning every 3 minutes, until the chicken is opaque with no trace of pink at the bone, 15 minutes.

THINK AHEAD
Marinate drumsticks up to 6 hours in advance. Cover and refrigerate.

LEMON GINGER CHICKEN DRUMSTICKS WITH MANGO AND MUSTARD SEED GLAZE

SERVES 4

8 chicken drumsticks, slashed
  (see page 102)

FOR MARINADE
2 tbsp grated fresh ginger
2 garlic cloves, crushed
½ tsp chili powder
juice of 1 lemon

FOR GLAZE
¼ cup jarred mango chutney, strained
1 tbsp yellow mustard seeds
salt

For marinade, combine ginger, garlic, chili powder, and lemon juice. Add drumsticks and toss to coat evenly. Cover and refrigerate for 30 minutes. For glaze, combine chutney and mustard seeds. Grill according to instructions below, brushing with glaze throughout. Sprinkle with salt. Serve hot.

OUTDOOR
Grill over medium hot coals , turning every 3 minutes, until the chicken is opaque with no trace of pink at the bone, 15 minutes.

INDOOR
Preheat broiler. Broil, turning every 3 minutes, until the chicken is opaque with no trace of pink at the bone, 15 minutes.

THINK AHEAD
Marinate drumsticks up to 4 hours in advance. Cover and refrigerate, turning several times in marinade.

BONING CHICKEN LEG

Place leg skin side down. With a small, sharp knife, cut down the thigh toward the leg joint to expose the thigh bone. Lift the bone, scraping and making small cuts to release the flesh from the bone.

Hold the released thigh bone, and cut around joint to free. With the tip of knife scrape down the length of the drumstick bone to expose, scraping and pushing the meat down and away from you. Stop scraping when you get to the knuckle end, at which stage you will have turned the chicken leg inside out.

With large chef's knife, cut off the bone about 1 inch from the knuckle end. Reshape the chicken leg by turning skin right side out again.

THINK AHEAD
Bone chicken leg up to 1 day in advance. Cover tightly with plastic wrap and refrigerate.

CHICKEN LEGS STUFFED WITH WILD MUSHROOMS

SERVES 4
4 chicken legs, boned (see left)
2 tsp salt
1 tsp black pepper
FOR STUFFING
1 tbsp olive oil
2 garlic cloves, crushed
4 shallots, finely chopped
1 tbsp fresh thyme leaves
2½ cups chopped fresh wild mushrooms (see below)
dash of brandy, optoinal
1 tsp white truffle oil, optional
salt, black pepper

extra olive oil for brushing

ESSENTIAL EQUIPMENT
4 - 10-inch presoaked bamboo skewers

Sprinkle salt and pepper inside chicken legs.
Heat oil in a skillet over high heat until hot but not smoking. Add garlic, shallots, thyme, and mushrooms. Stir fry until wilted and starting to crisp, 5 minutes. Add brandy. Stand back from pan and set alight with a long match. Allow flames to burn out, then remove pan from heat and leave to cool completely. Stir in truffle oil if using and add salt and pepper to taste. Place boned chicken legs skin side down. Using a tablespoon, push a quarter of the mushroom mixture inside each leg cavity. Use the back of the spoon to spread some of this mushroom mixture up onto the inside of the thigh. Wrap the thigh meat around the stuffing and reshape. Pull the skin over to seal and thread skewer through the thigh to secure flaps. Grill according to instructions below. Serve hot.

OUTDOOR
Grill over medium-hot coals, basting regularly, until meat is opaque and stuffing is cooked through, 7–10 minutes per side.

INDOOR
Preheat oven to 400°F. Brush chicken with olive oil and place on oven tray. Roast until cooked through, 20–25 minutes.

THINK AHEAD
Stuff chicken legs up to 6 hours in advance. Remove from refrigerator and bring to room temperature before placing on the grill.

COOKS' NOTE
Make sure that the mushroom mixture is completely cool before stuffing. Placing a hot mixture into uncooked chicken could present a health hazard when done ahead.
A bunch of herbs makes an aromatic alternative to a basting brush. Choose robust, woody herbs like thyme and rosemary.

WILD MUSHROOMS
There are many varieties of wild mushrooms. Field or shiitake mushrooms are excellent for this recipe. Field mushrooms have an open, flat cap with exposed brown gills and a strong, savory flavor. Shiitake mushrooms are a widely available Asian variety with a powerful meaty flavor. For a deluxe selection, choose from a mixture of chanterelles, porcini (also called cèpes), and morels.

To clean mushrooms, wipe clean with damp paper towels. Never wash or rinse mushrooms in water.

TARRAGON MUSTARD CHICKEN SKEWERS

SERVES 4

8 boneless, skinless chicken thighs	**1 tbsp sugar**
2 tbsp dried tarragon	**1 tsp black pepper**
¼ cup Dijon mustard	**salt**
¼ cup red wine vinegar	**1 recipe creamy blue cheese sauce (see page 133), optional**
2 tsp paprika	

ESSENTIAL EQUIPMENT
8 - 10-inch presoaked bamboo skewers

Cut each thigh into 6 equal-sized pieces. Thread onto skewers. Combine tarragon, mustard, vinegar, paprika, sugar, and pepper. Pour over skewered chicken. Cover and refrigerate for 30 minutes. Grill according to instructions below. Sprinkle with salt. Serve hot with creamy blue cheese sauce.

OUTDOOR
Grill over medium-hot coals until the chicken is opaque with no trace of pink, 5 minutes per side.

INDOOR
Preheat broiler. Broil until the chicken is opaque with no trace of pink, 5 minutes per side.

THINK AHEAD
Marinate chicken up to 4 hours in advance. Cover and refrigerate.

CURRIED COCONUT CHICKEN

SERVES 4

8 boneless, skinless chicken thighs	**1 tbsp garam masala mix (see page 25)**
4 garlic cloves, crushed	**½ cup coconut milk**
1 tbsp grated fresh ginger	**salt, black pepper**
1 onion, chopped	**1 recipe Asian noodle salad (see page 150), optional**
1 handful cilantro leaves	
3 tbsp fish sauce	

ESSENTIAL EQUIPMENT
16 - 10-inch presoaked bamboo skewers

Spread chicken thighs flat. Thread 2 skewers diagonally through each thigh, to form a cross. Place garlic, ginger, onion, cilantro, fish sauce, masala mix, and coconut milk in a food processor or blender; pulse until smooth. Pour mixture over chicken. Cover and refrigerate for 30 minutes. Grill according to instructions below. Sprinkle with salt and pepper. Serve hot with Asian noodle salad, optional.

OUTDOOR
Grill over medium-hot coals until chicken is opaque with no trace of pink, 5 minutes per side.

INDOOR
Preheat broiler. Broil until chicken is opaque with no trace of pink, 5 minutes per side.

THINK AHEAD
Marinate chicken up to 6 hours in advance. Cover and refrigerate.

COOKS' NOTE
Skewering chicken thighs keeps them flat and open on the grill, allowing them to cook evenly.

GINGER HOISIN CHICKEN SKEWERS

SERVES 4

8 boneless, skinless chicken thighs
2 garlic cloves, chopped
3 tbsp grated fresh ginger
1 tbsp Chinese hot chili sauce

1 tbsp soy sauce
1 tbsp dark brown sugar
¼ cup hoisin sauce
8 scallions, trimmed

ESSENTIAL EQUIPMENT
8 - 10-inch presoaked bamboo skewers

Cut thighs into 1-inch cubes. Combine garlic, ginger, chili sauce, soy sauce, sugar, and hoisin. Add chicken and toss to coat evenly. Cover and refrigerate for 30 minutes. Divide chicken cubes equally and skewer. Thread a scallion over either end of each skewer, to form a bow shape round the chicken pieces. Grill according to instructions below. Serve hot.

OUTDOOR
Grill over medium-hot coals until chicken is opaque with no trace of pink, 5 minutes per side.

INDOOR
Preheat broiler. Broil until chicken is opaque with no trace of pink, 5 minutes per side.

THINK AHEAD
Marinate chicken up to 4 hours in advance. Cover and refrigerate.

CARDAMOM CHICKEN TIKKA

SERVES 4

8 boneless, skinless chicken thighs
juice of 1 lemon
2 tsp black pepper
1 tbsp grated fresh ginger
3 garlic cloves, crushed
1 fresh green chile, seeded and
 finely chopped
1 tsp ground cardamom
½ tsp ground cumin

½ tsp ground nutmeg
1 tbsp heavy cream
3 tbsp Greek-style whole milk yogurt
 or sour cream
1½ lemons, cut into 8 wedges
salt
1 recipe cucumber yogurt raita
 (see page 138), optional

ESSENTIAL EQUIPMENT
8 - 10-inch presoaked bamboo skewers

Cut each thigh into 6 equal-sized pieces. Toss chicken pieces with lemon juice and pepper. Cover and refrigerate for 30 minutes. Drain lemon juice. Add ginger, garlic, chile, cardamom, cumin, nutmeg, cream, and yogurt or sour cream to chicken. Toss together to coat chicken well. Cover and refrigerate for 1 hour. Remove chicken cubes from marinade, shaking off any excess. Thread onto skewers with lemon wedges. Grill according to instructions below. Sprinkle with salt. Serve hot with cucumber yogurt raita, optional.

OUTDOOR
Grill over medium-hot coals until chicken is opaque with no trace of pink, 5 minutes per side.

INDOOR
Preheat broiler. Broil until the chicken is opaque with no trace of pink, 5 minutes per side.

THINK AHEAD
Marinate chicken up to 4 hours in advance. Cover and refrigerate.

COOKS' NOTE
It's best to grind the cardamom just before using, since its fragrance fades quickly after grinding. Lightly crush the pods to remove the grainlike seeds, then crush (see page 161) until finely ground.

TERIYAKI CHICKEN

SERVES 4

¼ cup shoyu (Japanese soy sauce)
2 tbsp mirin
¼ cup sake
1 tbsp sugar
8 boneless, skinless chicken thighs

ESSENTIAL EQUIPMENT
*8 attached pairs presoaked wooden chopsticks
or 8 - 10-inch presoaked bamboo skewers*

Combine shoyu, mirin, sake, and sugar in small pan over medium heat. Bring to a boil, stirring to dissolve the sugar. Lower heat and simmer until thick and syrupy, 5–10 minutes. Cool. Set aside half the sauce for glazing the chicken. Reserve remaining half to drizzle over before serving. Cut each thigh into 3 even-sized pieces. Insert the blade of a small, sharp knife through the middle of each chicken piece to make a slit. Thread 3 slit pieces onto each pair of attached chopsticks. Brush all over with the cooled sauce to glaze. Grill according to instructions below, basting with sauce. Drizzle with reserved sauce. Serve hot.

OUTDOOR
Grill over medium hot coals until the chicken is opaque with no trace of pink, 7 minutes per side.

INDOOR
Preheat broiler. Broil until the chicken is opaque with no trace of pink, 7 minutes per side.

THINK AHEAD
Make sauce up to 3 days in advance. Cover and refrigerate.

COOKS' NOTE
We like to serve teriyaki chicken on pairs of chopsticks for a fun and impressive presentation. Since they do not have sharpened ends, use a knife to make an incision through the chicken to help you slide the chicken pieces onto the chopsticks. Alternatively, use presoaked bamboo skewers.

SPLITTING POULTRY

Place bird breast side down. With kitchen scissors or poultry shears, cut along each side of the backbone. Remove and discard.

Snip the wishbone and cut ½ inch into the breast bone so that the bird can be pressed flat

THINK AHEAD
Split bird up to 1 day in advance. Cover tightly with plastic wrap and refrigerate.

COOKS' NOTE
Splitting is a useful technique for the grill. Opening the birds flat and making them an equal thickness allows for quick, even cooking. The meat is cooked throughout without drying out.

We prefer to start cooking split birds bone side down since the heat of the grill takes longer to penetrate the denser, bony side. You can turn your attention to coloring the skin side nicely once you are sure that the bird is on its way to being cooked through.

LEMON-PEPPERED ROCK CORNISH GAME HENS

SERVES 4

4 rock cornish game hens, split (see left)
1 lemon, peeled and chopped (see page 161)
2 tsp crushed red pepper flakes
2 garlic cloves, crushed

2 tbsp Worcestershire sauce
¼ cup peanut oil
salt, black pepper
1 recipe roasted garlic aïoli (see page 143), optional

ESSENTIAL EQUIPMENT
8 - 14-inch flat metal skewers

Place a game hen cut side down and press flat. Push a skewer horizontally through the wings and breast. Push another skewer horizontally through the thighs. Repeat with remaining game hens.
Combine lemon, red pepper flakes, garlic, Worcestershire sauce, and oil in a large dish. Add game hens, turning to coat both sides. Cover and refrigerate for 30 minutes. Grill according to instructions below. Remove skewers. Sprinkle with salt and pepper. Serve hot with roasted garlic aïoli, optional.

OUTDOOR
Grill bone side down over medium-hot coals for 15 minutes. Turn and grill skin side down until skin is crispy and there is no trace of pink at the bone, 10 minutes.

INDOOR
Preheat broiler. Broil bone side up for 15 minutes. Turn and cook skin side up until skin is crispy and there is no trace of pink at the bone, 10 minutes.

THINK AHEAD
Marinate game hens up to 3 hours in advance. Cover and refrigerate, turning several times.

GAME HEN VARIATION

SPICY JERK GAME HENS

Replace lemon, red pepper flakes, garlic, Worcestershire sauce, and oil with spicy jerk rub (see page 24). Omit roasted garlic aïoli when serving.

SCORING DUCK SKIN

With a sharp knife, cut diagonal parallel slashes ½ inch apart through skin to make a diamond pattern. Be careful not to pierce the flesh.

COOKS' NOTE
Scoring is essential if you want perfectly crisp duck. The scored surface allows the layer of fat under the skin to melt away so that the outer skin can crisp.

CRISPY BALSAMIC DUCK

SERVES 4
5 tbsp balsamic vinegar
4 duck breast halves, scored (see left)
salt, black pepper
1 tbsp extra balsamic vinegar for drizzling

Put 5 tbsp vinegar in a shallow dish just wide enough to fit 4 breast halves. Add the duck breast halves, skin side up. Cover and let marinate for 20 minutes at room temperature. Grill or roast according to instructions below. Cover with foil and leave to rest for 5 minutes before cutting into thin slices (see below). Sprinkle with salt and pepper. Drizzle with remaining balsamic vinegar. Serve hot.

OUTDOOR
Grill over medium coals, skin side down until the skin is crispy, 5 minutes. Turn and grill for further 8 minutes for medium rare, 10 minutes for well done.

INDOOR
Preheat oven to 400°F. Preheat a heavy ovenproof skillet over medium heat. Add duck skin side down and cook until crispy, 5 minutes. Turn breasts and place pan in the oven for 8 minutes for medium rare, 10 minutes for well done.

THINK AHEAD
Marinate duck breasts up to 2 hours in advance. Cover and refrigerate.

COOKS' NOTE
We like to serve this tangy duck dish with a slice of roasted onion focaccia with rosemary (see page 155).

SPICED SOY DUCK

SERVES 4

2 tbsp honey
1 tbsp soy sauce
½ tsp Chinese five-spice powder
4 duck breast halves, scored
  (see page 111)

Combine honey, soy sauce, and spice.
Put mixture in a shallow dish just wide
enough to fit 4 breast halves. Add the
duck breast halves, skin side up. Cover
and let marinate for 20 minutes at room
temperature. Grill or roast according to
instructions below. Cover with foil and
leave to rest for 5 minutes before slicing
across on the diagonal. Serve hot.

OUTDOOR
Grill over medium coals,
skin side down until the
skin is crispy, 5 minutes.
Turn and grill for another
8 minutes for medium
rare, 10 minutes for
well done.

INDOOR
Preheat oven to 400°F.
Preheat a heavy
ovenproof skillet over
medium heat. Add duck
skin side down and cook
until crispy,
5 minutes. Turn breasts
and place pan in the
oven for 8 minutes for
medium rare, 10
minutes for well done.

THINK AHEAD
Marinate duck breasts up to 2 hours in advance.
Cover and refrigerate.

COOKS' NOTE
Fresh papaya sambal (see page 137) and sesame
soba noodle salad (see page 148) are both delicious
accompaniments to this spicy duck.

DUCK WITH SWEET ORANGE GLAZE

SERVES 4

juice of 2 oranges   **salt, black pepper**
2 tbsp honey
4 duck breast halves, scored
  (see page 111)

For glaze, combine 2 tbsp of the orange juice with the honey.
Put remaining orange juice in shallow dish just wide enough for 4 breast halves.
Add the duck breast halves, skin side up. Cover and let marinate for 20 minutes at
room temperature. Grill or roast according to instructions below, basting with glaze
throughout. Cover with foil and leave to rest for 5 minutes before cutting on the
diagonal into thin slices. Sprinkle with salt and pepper. Serve hot.

OUTDOOR
Grill over medium coals, skin side down until the
skin is crispy, 5 minutes. Turn and grill for another
8 minutes for medium rare, 10 minutes for well done.

INDOOR
Preheat oven to 400°F. Preheat a heavy ovenproof
skillet over medium heat. Add duck skin side down
and cook until crispy, 5 minutes. Turn breasts and
place pan in the oven for 8 minutes for medium rare,
10 minutes for well done.

THINK AHEAD
Marinate duck breasts up to 2 hours in advance. Cover and refrigerate.

COOKS' NOTE
A crisp, green-leaf salad with honey mustard dressing (see page 152) is the perfect match for this succulent,
savory duck.

CINNAMON QUAIL WITH POMEGRANATE GLAZE

SERVES 4

8 quail, split (see page 110)
1 tsp ground cinnamon
2 tbsp pomegranate molasses
1 tbsp olive oil
salt, black pepper

ESSENTIAL EQUIPMENT
8 - 14-inch flat metal skewers

Place 2 quail cut side down and press flat. Push a skewer horizontally through the wings and breast of both quail. Push another skewer horizontally through the thighs. Repeat with remaining quail. Combine cinnamon and pomegranate molasses and rub over quail. Cover with plastic wrap and refrigerate for 30 minutes. Remove from refrigerator and bring to room temperature. Drizzle with oil. Grill according to instructions below. Sprinkle with salt and pepper. Serve hot.

OUTDOOR
Grill bone side down over medium-hot coals for 8 minutes. Turn and grill skin side down, until the meat is opaque and there is no trace of pink at the bone, another 5 minutes.

INDOOR
Preheat broiler. Broil bone side up for 8 minutes. Turn and cook skin side up until skin is crispy and there is no trace of pink at the bone, another 5 minutes.

THINK AHEAD
Marinate quail up to 4 hours in advance. Cover and refrigerate.

COOKS' NOTE
Pomegranate molasses—also referred to as syrup and concentrate—is made by boiling down pomegranate juice to a thick dark brown liquid with a distinctive sweet sour flavor. It's a favorite flavoring across the Middle East but especially in Iran, Syria, and Lebanon. Look for it in Middle-Eastern shops or order it from a gourmet mail order company (see page 167). Alternatively, use date molasses, which is available in health food stores.

ROSEMARY GARLIC QUAIL

SERVES 4

8 quail, split (see page 110)
1 tsp dried rosemary
2 garlic cloves, crushed
½ tsp black pepper
¼ tsp crushed red pepper flakes
1 tbsp fresh lemon juice
1 tbsp olive oil

ESSENTIAL EQUIPMENT
8 - 14-inch flat metal skewers

Place 2 quail cut side down and press flat. Push a skewer horizontally through the wings and breast of both quail. Push another skewer horizontally through the thighs. Repeat with remaining quail and skewers. Combine rosemary, garlic, pepper, red pepper flakes, lemon juice, and oil. Let mixture stand at room temperature for 30 minutes to allow flavors to combine. Brush mixture over quail. Grill according to instructions below, basting throughout with remaining mixture. Sprinkle with salt. Serve hot.

OUTDOOR
Grill bone side down over medium-hot coals for 8 minutes. Turn and grill skin side down, until the meat is opaque and there is no trace of pink at the bone, another 5 minutes.

INDOOR
Preheat broiler. Broil bone side up for 8 minutes. Turn and grill skin side up until skin is crispy and there is no trace of pink at the bone, another 5 minutes.

THINK AHEAD
Make marinade up to 1 day in advance. Cover and store at room temperature.

COOKS' NOTE
The intense, sun-filled flavors of slow roasted tomato salad (see page 147) perfectly complement these grilled Tuscan-style quails. This aromatic and spicy marinade is also delicious with split game hens (see page 110 for cooking times).

VEGETABLES & FRUIT ON THE GRILL

CHARGRILLED BALSAMIC RED ONIONS

SERVES 4
2 large red onions
2 tbsp olive oil
1 tbsp balsamic vinegar
salt, black pepper
1 tbsp each extra olive oil and balsamic vinegar to drizzle
1 tsp fresh thyme leaves

ESSENTIAL EQUIPMENT
4 - 14-inch flat metal skewers

Trim off and discard the root and stalk ends of the onions. Cut each onion into ¾-inch slices. Thread slices onto skewers. Brush both sides of each skewered slice with oil. Sprinkle with balsamic vinegar, salt, and pepper. Grill according to instructions below. Drizzle with remaining oil and vinegar. Sprinkle with thyme. Serve hot.

OUTDOOR
Grill over medium coals until tender and lightly charred, 5 minutes per side.

INDOOR
Preheat broiler. Broil until lightly charred, 5 minutes per side.

CHAR-ROASTED ROSEMARY ONIONS

SERVES 4
4 unpeeled large yellow or red onions
2 tbsp red wine or sherry vinegar
2 tbsp olive oil
salt, black pepper
1 tsp finely chopped fresh rosemary leaves
2 tbsp olive oil to drizzle
½ tbsp fresh rosemary leaves

Preheat oven to 350°F.
Cut onions in half from top to bottom. Trim and peel each onion half, leaving the root end attached to allow the onion halves to stay intact when cooking. Arrange onion halves on an oven tray, cut side up. Sprinkle evenly with vinegar, oil, salt, pepper, and chopped rosemary. Cover with foil and pre-roast for 30 minutes. Grill according to instructions below. Drizzle with olive oil and sprinkle with rosemary leaves. Serve hot.

OUTDOOR
Grill over medium-hot coals until lightly charred, 5 minutes per side.

INDOOR
Preheat broiler. Broil until lightly charred, 5 minutes per side.

THINK AHEAD
Preroast onions in oven up to 1 day in advance. Cover and store at room temperature.

COOKS' NOTE
These onions make a great vegetarian main course when served with creamy blue-cheese sauce (see page 133).

CHARGRILLED CORN ON THE COB WITH CILANTRO CHILI BUTTER

SERVES 4

4 ears fresh corn
2 tbsp melted butter
salt, black pepper
4 - ¾-inch slices cilantro chili butter
  (see page 140)
lime wedges

Cook corn in unsalted boiling water for 2 minutes. Refresh in cold water. Brush with melted butter. Grill according to instructions below. Sprinkle with salt and pepper. Serve each ear hot with a slice of cilantro chili butter and a wedge of lime.

OUTDOOR
Grill over medium-hot coals, turning frequently, until lightly charred, 5 minutes.

INDOOR
Preheat broiler. Broil, turning frequently until lightly charred, 5 minutes.

THINK AHEAD
Boil corn up to 1 day in advance. Refresh immediately in cold water. Cover and refrigerate. Grill just before serving.

COOKS' NOTE
We also love chargrilled corn on the cob spread with roasted garlic aïoli (see page 143).

CHAR-ROASTED PEPPERS

SERVES 4

3 red, yellow, or orange peppers
1 tbsp balsamic vinegar
3 tbsp olive oil
salt, black pepper

Grill peppers whole according to instructions below. Place grilled peppers in a plastic bag or a bowl with a plate on top. Leave for 5–10 minutes until cool enough to handle. Uncover and peel off charred skin. Discard stems and seeds (see page 160). Slice peppers into ½-inch-wide strips. Toss strips with vinegar and oil. Add salt and pepper to taste. Serve warm or at room temperature.

OUTDOOR
Grill over flaming coals, turning frequently, until skin is charred all over, 10 minutes.

INDOOR
Preheat broiler. Place under broiler, turning frequently, until skin is charred all over, 10 minutes.

THINK AHEAD
Grill peppers up to 1 day in advance. Store covered at room temperature.

CHARGRILLED NEW POTATO SKEWERS

SERVES 4

1½ lbs unpeeled new potatoes
3 tbsp olive oil
salt, black pepper

ESSENTIAL EQUIPMENT
4 - 10-inch presoaked bamboo skewers

Cook potatoes in boiling salted water until just tender, 15 minutes. Cut in half and toss with oil, salt, and pepper. Thread potato halves onto skewers. Grill according to instructions below. Serve hot.

OUTDOOR
Grill over medium coals, turning regularly, until lightly charred, 10 minutes.

INDOOR
Preheat broiler. Broil, turning regularly, until lightly charred, 10 minutes.

THINK AHEAD
Precook potatoes up to 1 day in advance. Cut in half, toss in oil, and skewer up to 2 hours in advance. Cover and keep at room temperature until ready to grill.

CHARGRILLED TOMATOES

SERVES 4

4 ripe tomatoes, halved
1 tbsp olive oil
salt, black pepper

Place tomato halves skin side down. Sprinkle with oil, salt, and pepper. Grill according to instructions below. Serve hot or at room temperature.

OUTDOOR
Grill over medium-hot coals until lightly charred on the outside but still firm, 3 minutes per side.

INDOOR
Preheat broiler. Broil until lightly charred on the outside but still firm, 3 minutes per side.

CHARGRILLED GARLIC POTATO SLICES

SERVES 4

1½ lbs unpeeled plain or sweet potatoes, sliced
½ inch thick
2 garlic cloves, crushed
¼ cup olive oil
salt, black pepper
1 recipe roasted garlic aïoli (see page 143), optional

Cook potato slices in boiling salted water until tender but still firm, 5 minutes. Drain. Combine the garlic and oil. Brush potato slices with garlic oil. Grill according to instructions below. Sprinkle with salt and pepper. Serve hot with aïoli, optional.

OUTDOOR
Grill over medium coals until lightly charred, 5 minutes per side.

INDOOR
Preheat broiler. Broil until lightly charred, 5 minutes per side.

THINK AHEAD
Boil potato slices up to 4 hours in advance. Cool, cover, and keep at room temperature until ready to grill.

CHARGRILLED EGGPLANT SLICES WITH LEMON TAHINI SAUCE

SERVES 4

2 eggplants, cut into ¹/₂-inch-thick slices
½ cup olive oil
salt, black pepper
1 recipe lemon tahini sauce (see page 132)

Brush the eggplant slices on both sides with olive oil. Grill according to instructions below. Sprinkle with salt and pepper. Serve hot or at room temperature with lemon tahini sauce.

OUTDOOR
Grill over medium-hot coals until lightly charred and tender, 5 minutes per side.

INDOOR
Preheat a ridged cast-iron grill pan over high heat. Cook until lightly charred and tender, 5 minutes per side.

THINK AHEAD
Grill eggplants up to 6 hours in advance. Cover and store at room temperature.

COOKS' NOTE
Salsa verde (see page 134), charmoula (see page 23), spicy peanut sauce (see page 136), roasted pepper and basil salsa (see page 138), or spiced chickpea sauce (see page 137) are all excellent choices to serve with these eggplant slices in place of the lemon tahini sauce.

CHAR-ROASTED EGGPLANT WITH SESAME AND HONEY MISO GLAZE

SERVES 4

¼ cup honey miso sauce (see page 138)
2 tbsp sesame seeds
2 eggplants
extra honey miso sauce for drizzling

For glaze, combine honey miso sauce and sesame seeds. Prick eggplants all over with fork. Grill according to instructions below. Cut in half lengthwise. Return halved eggplant to the grill and cook, cut side down, until grill marks appear. Brush scored side with glaze. Grill glazed cut side down until sizzling and tender, another 5 minutes. Serve hot with extra honey miso sauce drizzled over.

OUTDOOR
Grill over medium coals, turning frequently until charred all over, 15 minutes. Leave until cool enough to handle, about 10 minutes.

INDOOR
Preheat broiler. Broil, turning frequently, until charred all over, 15 minutes. Leave until cool enough to handle, about 10 minutes.

EGGPLANT VARIATION

CHAR-ROASTED EGGPLANT WITH SPICY PEANUT SAUCE

SERVES 4

Omit honey miso sauce and sesame seeds. Spread scored side of eggplant with 4 tbsp spicy peanut sauce (see page 136). Serve with remaining spicy peanut sauce.

CHARGRILLED ZUCCHINI WITH ROASTED PEPPER AND BASIL SALSA

SERVES 4

1lb zucchini, sliced ½-inch-thick lengthwise
3 tbsp olive oil
salt, black pepper
1 recipe roasted pepper and basil salsa (see page 138)

Grill zucchini according to instructions below. Arrange on platter. Top with salsa and serve hot or at room temperature.

OUTDOOR
Grill over medium coals until lightly charred and tender, 5–10 minutes per side.

INDOOR
Preheat a ridged cast-iron grill pan over high heat. Cook until lightly charred and tender, 5–10 minutes per side.

COOKS' NOTE
This makes a great vegetarian main course when served with radish tzatziki (see page 135) or creamy blue-cheese sauce (see page 133).

CHARGRILLED SQUASH WITH JERKED HONEY RUM GLAZE

SERVES 4

1lb unpeeled butternut squash, cut into
½-inch-thick slices
thick slices
1 recipe jerked honey rum glaze (see page 25)
salt, black pepper

Bring a large pan of water to the boil. Add squash slices and when water returns to rolling boil, drain. Arrange in a single layer on a dish towel and pat dry. Grill according to instructions below. Sprinkle with salt and pepper and serve hot.

OUTDOOR
Grill over medium-hot coals, brushing with glaze and turning once until lightly charred, 3 minutes per side.

INDOOR
Preheat broiler. Brush with glaze and broil until browned, 3 minutes per side.

THINK AHEAD
Precook squash up to 4 hours in advance. Cover and leave at room temperature until ready to grill.

CHARGRILLED NECTARINES

SERVES 4
4 nectarines, halved and pitted
1 tbsp honey
vanilla ice cream

Brush cut sides of nectarine halves with honey. Grill according to instructions below. Serve hot with a scoop of vanilla ice cream.

OUTDOOR
Grill cut side down over medium-low coals until warm and lightly charred, but still firm, 5 minutes.

INDOOR
Preheat broiler. Broil cut side up until warm and lightly charred, but still firm, 5 minutes.

CHARGRILLED PINEAPPLE WITH SWEET RUM GLAZE

SERVES 4
1 unpeeled medium pineapple, quartered
2 tbsp dark rum
1 tbsp fresh lime juice
2 tbsp honey

Cut away the core from the pineapple quarters. For glaze, combine rum, lime juice, and honey and stir to dissolve. Grill according to instructions below. Serve hot with any remaining glaze drizzled over.

OUTDOOR
Grill over medium-low coals, brushing with glaze, until hot and lightly charred, 5–10 minutes per side.

INDOOR
Preheat broiler. Brush with glaze and broil until hot and lightly charred, 5–10 minutes per side.

VARIATION

CHARGRILLED PINEAPPLE WITH JERKED HONEY RUM GLAZE

Replace sweet rum glaze with jerked honey rum glaze (see page 25).

GRILL-ROASTED CINNAMON RUM BANANAS

SERVES 4

4 large bananas, cut on diagonal into 1-inch slices
juice of 1 lime
1 tbsp brown sugar
2 tbsp dark rum
1 tsp ground cinnamon
vanilla ice cream

ESSENTIAL EQUIPMENT
4 - 12-inch squares of extra thick or heavy duty foil

Toss banana slices with lime juice, sugar, rum, and cinnamon. Divide bananas among foil squares. Bring the edges of foil together and scrunch to seal. Grill roast according to instructions below. Serve warm with a scoop of vanilla ice cream.

OUTDOOR
Grill over medium-low coals until hot through, 15–20 minutes.

INDOOR
Preheat oven to 400°F. Bake until hot through, 10–15 minutes.

THINK AHEAD
Assemble foil packets up to 1 hour in advance. Store at room temperature.

GRILL-ROASTED LEMON LIQUEUR STRAWBERRIES

SERVES 4

1lb (3½ cups halved) strawberries, hulled and halved
3 tbsp grand marnier
grated zest of 1 lemon
2 tbsp sugar
vanilla ice cream

ESSENTIAL EQUIPMENT
4 - 12-inch squares of extra thick or heavy duty foil

Toss strawberry halves with grand marnier, lemon zest, and sugar. Divide strawberries among foil squares. Bring the edges of foil together and scrunch to seal. Grill roast according to instructions below. Serve warm with a scoop of vanilla ice cream.

OUTDOOR
Grill over medium-low coals until warm through, 5–10 minutes.

INDOOR
Preheat oven to 400°F. Bake until warm through, 5 minutes.

THINK AHEAD
Assemble foil packets up to 1 hour in advance. Store at room temperature.

GRILL-ROASTED SWEET SPICED ORANGES

SERVES 4

4 oranges, peeled (see page 161) and cut into 1-inch slices
1½ tbsp brown sugar
2 tsp brandy
1 tsp cardamom pods (about 12 pods)

ESSENTIAL EQUIPMENT
4 - 12-inch squares of extra thick or heavy duty foil

Toss orange slices with sugar and brandy. Divide orange slices among foil squares. Sprinkle with cardamom pods. Bring the edges of foil together and scrunch to seal. Grill roast according to instructions below. Serve hot.

OUTDOOR
Grill over medium-low coals until hot through, 15–20 minutes.

INDOOR
Preheat oven to 400°F. Bake until hot through, 10–15 minutes.

THINK AHEAD
Assemble foil packets up to 2 hours in advance. Store at room temperature.

GRILL-ROASTED HONEY ORANGE FIGS

SERVES 4

8 figs, halved
¼ cup honey
juice of 1 orange
grated zest of 1 orange
¼ cup mascarpone or crème fraîche

ESSENTIAL EQUIPMENT
4 - 12-inch squares of extra thick or heavy duty foil

Divide fig halves cut side up among foil squares. Drizzle with honey and orange juice and sprinkle with zest. Bring the edges of foil together and scrunch to seal. Grill roast according to instructions below. Serve hot with mascarpone or crème fraîche.

OUTDOOR
Grill over medium-low coals until hot through, 15–20 minutes.

INDOOR
Preheat oven to 400°F. Bake until hot through, 10–15 minutes.

THINK AHEAD
Assemble foil packets up to 2 hours in advance. Store at room temperature.

CHARGRILLED QUESADILLAS WITH SPICY CILANTRO

SERVES 4

1 handful cilantro leaves
2 garlic cloves, crushed
1 green chile, seeded and finely chopped
4 scallions, chopped
½ tsp ground coriander
½ tsp ground cumin
2 tbsp fresh lime juice
½ cup olive oil
salt, black pepper
8 8-inch flour tortillas
2½ cups grated Monterey Jack cheese
1 recipe avocado mango salsa (see page 136)
⅔ cup sour cream, optional

Place fresh cilantro, garlic, chile, scallions, ground coriander, cumin, lime juice, and oil in a food processor or blender; pulse to a smooth paste. Add salt and pepper to taste. Spread a quarter of the cilantro paste over 1 tortilla. Top evenly with a quarter of the cheese. Lightly press a second tortilla on top. Repeat with remaining tortillas, salsa, and cheese. Grill according to instructions below. Cut into wedges with kitchen scissors or a sharp serrated knife. Serve hot with avocado mango salsa and sour cream spooned over each wedge.

OUTDOOR
Grill over medium-hot coals until lightly charred and the cheese is melted, 2 minutes per side.

INDOOR
Preheat a ridged cast-iron grill pan over high heat. Cook until lightly charred and the cheese is melted, 2 minutes per side.

THINK AHEAD
Assemble tortillas up to 4 hours in advance. Cover with plastic wrap and leave at room temperature until ready to grill.

CHARGRILLED QUESADILLAS WITH SALSA FRESCA

SERVES 4

8 8-inch flour tortillas
1⅛ cup grated Monterey Jack cheese
1 recipe salsa fresca (see page 133)
1½ cups crumbled feta or queso fresco cheese
1 recipe creamy avocado salsa (see page 132), optional

Spread a quarter of the Monterey Jack over 1 tortilla. Top evenly with a quarter of the salsa fresca. Sprinkle with a quarter of the feta or queso fresco. Lightly press a second tortilla on top. Repeat with remaining tortillas, Monterey Jack, salsa, and feta or queso fresco. Grill according to instructions below. Cut into wedges with kitchen scissors or a sharp serrated knife. Serve hot with creamy avocado salsa spooned over each wedge, if desired.

OUTDOOR
Grill over medium-hot coals until lightly charred and the jack cheese is melted, 2 minutes per side.

INDOOR
Preheat a ridged cast-iron grill pan over high heat. Cook until lightly charred and the jack cheese is melted, 2 minutes per side.

THINK AHEAD
Assemble tortillas up to 4 hours in advance. Cover with plastic wrap and leave at room temperature until ready to grill.

CHARGRILLED EGGPLANT, GOAT CHEESE, AND MINT BRUSCHETTA

SERVES 4

8 slices day old ciabatta or country-style bread, ½ inch thick
1 medium eggplant, cut crosswise into ½-inch-thick slices
¼ cup olive oil for brushing

FOR DRESSING
1 tbsp finely chopped fresh mint leaves
1 tbsp balsamic vinegar
1 tbsp olive oil
salt, black pepper

½ cup fresh creamy goat cheese
extra olive oil for drizzling

Toast bread slices until crisp, about 2 minutes per side.
Brush the eggplant slices on both sides with olive oil. Grill according to instructions below. Toss eggplant slices gently with mint, vinegar, and oil. Sprinkle with salt and pepper to taste. Spread bruschetta with equal amounts of goat's cheese. Top with eggplant and drizzle with extra olive oil. Serve at room temperature.

OUTDOOR
Grill over medium-hot coals until lightly charred and tender, 5 minutes per side.

INDOOR
Preheat a ridged cast-iron grill pan over high heat. Cook until lightly charred and tender, 5 minutes per side.

THINK AHEAD
Toast bruschetta up to 1 day in advance. Store in an airtight container at room temperature. Grill eggplant up to 6 hours in advance. Leave covered at room temperature until ready to serve.

CHAR-ROASTED LEMON OREGANO PEPPERS ON BRUSCHETTA

SERVES 4

8 slices of day old ciabatta or country-style bread, ½ inch thick
3 red peppers
2 tbsp fresh lemon juice

2 garlic cloves, crushed
2 tsp finely chopped fresh oregano
5 tbsp olive oil
salt, black pepper

Toast bread slices until crisp, 2 minutes per side.
Grill peppers according to instructions below. Place grilled peppers in a plastic bag or a bowl with a plate on top. Leave for 5–10 minutes until cool enough to handle. Uncover and peel off charred skin (see page 160). Discard stems and seeds (see page 160). Slice peppers into ½-inch-wide strips. Toss strips with lemon, garlic, oregano, and oil. Add salt and pepper to taste. Top bruschetta with equal amounts of dressed peppers. Serve warm or at room temperature.

OUTDOOR
Grill over flaming coals, turning frequently, until skin is charred all over, 10 minutes.

INDOOR
Preheat broiler. Place under broiler, turning frequently, until skin is charred all over, 10 minutes.

THINK AHEAD
Prepare bruschetta and peppers up to one day in advance. Store bruschetta in an airtight container at room temperature. Store peppers separately at room temperature.

CREAMY AVOCADO SALSA

MAKES 2⅛ CUPS

2 avocados, peeled, halved, and pitted
6 scallions, chopped
1 handful cilantro leaves
2 tbsp red wine vinegar
2 tbsp olive oil
1 cup sour cream
salt, black pepper

Place avocado, scallions, cilantro, vinegar, oil, and sour cream
in a food processor or blender; pulse to a smooth purée. Add
salt and pepper to taste. Cover and refrigerate for 30 minutes
to allow flavors to blend. Serve chilled.

THINK AHEAD
Make salsa up to 1 day in advance. Cover and refrigerate.

COOKS' NOTE
To prevent discoloration, store in a bowl with plastic wrap, pressing directly on the
salsa to prevent contact with air.

LEMON TAHINI SAUCE

MAKES 1 CUP

⅓ cup tahini
1 garlic clove, crushed
juice of 1 lemon
½ cup water
salt, black pepper

Whisk tahini, garlic, and lemon juice together until smooth.
Whisk in water. Add salt and pepper to taste. Cover and let
stand at room temperature for 30 minutes to allow flavors to
blend. Serve chilled or at room temperature.

THINK AHEAD
Make sauce up to 2 days in advance. Cover and refrigerate.

CREAMY BLUE-CHEESE SAUCE

MAKES 2⅛ CUPS

6 scallions, chopped
7oz blue cheese
1¼ cups sour cream
1 tsp Worcestershire sauce
salt, black pepper

Place scallions, cheese, cream, and worcestershire sauce in a food processor or blender; pulse until smooth. Add salt and pepper to taste. Cover and refrigerate for 30 minutes to allow flavors to blend. Serve chilled.

THINK AHEAD
Make sauce up to 1 day in advance. Cover and refrigerate. Let stand at room temperature for 15 minutes to soften slightly before serving.

SALSA FRESCA

MAKES ABOUT 1⅔ CUPS

6 medium tomatoes, seeded (see page 161) and
finely diced
1 red onion, finely chopped
2 garlic cloves, crushed
1 fresh green chile, seeded and finely chopped
1 tbsp fresh lime juice
2 tbsp olive oil
2 tbsp finely chopped cilantro leaves
salt, black pepper

Combine tomatoes, onion, garlic, chile, lime juice, oil, and cilantro. Add salt and pepper to taste. Cover and let stand for 30 minutes at room temperature to allow flavors to blend. Serve chilled or at room temperature.

THINK AHEAD
Make salsa up to 1 day in advance. Cover and refrigerate.

SALSA VERDE

MAKES ¾ CUP

2 handfuls flat-leaf parsley leaves
10 fresh basil leaves
10 fresh mint leaves
1 garlic clove, crushed
1 tbsp Dijon mustard
1 tbsp drained capers
2 anchovy fillets
½ tsp red wine vinegar
⅔ cup olive oil
salt, black pepper

Place parsley, basil, mint, garlic, mustard, capers, anchovy, vinegar, and oil in a food processor or blender; pulse to a purée. Add salt and pepper to taste. Cover and let stand for 30 minutes at room temperature to allow flavors to blend. Serve at room temperature.

THINK AHEAD
Make salsa up to 3 days in advance. Cover and refrigerate. Bring to room temperature and stir before serving.

PINEAPPLE LIME SALSA

MAKES 1⅔ CUPS

½ fresh pineapple, cored
  and finely diced
1 fresh red chile, seeded
  and finely chopped
1 red onion, finely chopped
2 tbsp finely chopped cilantro
  or mint leaves
grated zest 1 lime
3 tbsp fresh lime juice
salt, tabasco

Combine pineapple, chile, onion, cilantro or mint, lime zest, and lime juice. Add salt and tabasco to taste. Cover and let stand for 30 minutes at room temperature to allow flavors to blend. Serve chilled or at room temperature.

THINK AHEAD
Make salsa up to 3 hours in advance. Cover and refrigerate.

COOKS' NOTE
A serrated knife is the best tool for cutting away the peel from a fresh pineapple. Cut off the leaves at their base and the bottom rind first. Stand the pineapple on its base and cut off the rind from the sides, using downward strokes.

RADISH TZATZIKI

MAKES 2⅛ CUPS

1½ cups radishes, grated
1 red onion, grated
2 garlic cloves, crushed
1 tbsp red wine vinegar
1 tsp sugar
¾ cup Greek-style whole milk yogurt or
   sour cream
salt, black pepper

Combine radishes, onion, garlic, vinegar, sugar, and yogurt or sour cream. Add salt and pepper to taste. Cover and refrigerate for 30 minutes to allow flavors to blend. Serve chilled.

THINK AHEAD
Make tzatziki up to 1 day in advance. Cover and refrigerate. Stir before serving.

CHIMI CHURRI

MAKES ¾ CUP

2 handfuls parsley leaves
4 scallions, chopped
8 garlic cloves, crushed
½ tsp crushed red pepper
   flakes
1 tsp dried oregano
¼ cup red wine
   vinegar
½ cup canola oil
salt, black pepper

Place parsley, scallions, garlic, red pepper flakes, oregano, vinegar, and oil in a food processor or blender; pulse until well blended but still retaining some texture. Add salt and pepper to taste. Cover and let stand for 30 minutes at room temperature to allow flavors to blend. Serve chilled or at room temperature.

THINK AHEAD
Make up to 3 days in advance, but add the vinegar just 2 hours before serving.

COOKS' NOTE
When making this colorful sauce more than a couple of hours in advance, be sure to follow the instructions for adding vinegar at a later time. If added too far in advance, the vinegar will "cook" the parsley, causing the vibrant green color of the sauce to fade.

AVOCADO MANGO SALSA

MAKES 1⅔ CUPS

1 mango, finely diced
1 avocado, peeled, halved, pitted, and finely diced
½ red onion, finely chopped
1 red chile, seeded and finely chopped
1 tbsp fresh lime juice
1 tbsp red wine vinegar
2 tbsp olive oil
2 tbsp finely chopped mint leaves
salt, tabasco

Combine mango, avocado, onion, chile, lime juice, vinegar, oil, and mint. Add salt and tabasco to taste. Cover and let stand for 30 minutes at room temperature to allow flavors to blend. Serve chilled or at room temperature.

THINK AHEAD
Make salsa up to 6 hours before serving. Cover and refrigerate.

COOKS' NOTE
To prevent discoloration, store in a bowl with plastic wrap, pressing directly on the salsa to prevent contact with air.

SPICY PEANUT SAUCE

MAKES 2⅛ CUPS

1 cup peanut butter
2 garlic cloves, crushed
1 tbsp grated fresh ginger
1 tsp turmeric
1 tsp tabasco
1 tbsp toasted sesame oil
4 tbsp soy sauce
2 tbsp honey
juice of 1 lemon
½ cup water

Place peanut butter, garlic, ginger, turmeric, tabasco, oil, soy sauce, honey, lemon juice, and water in a food processor or blender; pulse until smooth. Cover and let stand for 30 minutes at room temperature to allow flavors to blend. Serve chilled or at room temperature.

THINK AHEAD
Make sauce up to 3 days in advance. Cover and refrigerate.

COOKS' NOTE
For a spicy peanut dip with an extra rich coconut flavor, replace the water with an equal amount of coconut milk.

FRESH PAPAYA SAMBAL

MAKES ABOUT 1 CUP

1 papaya, seeded and finely chopped
½ red onion, finely chopped
1 tbsp finely chopped cilantro leaves
2 tbsp fresh lime juice
1 tbsp fish sauce
1 tsp sugar
salt, black pepper

Combine papaya, onion, cilantro, lime juice, fish sauce, and sugar. Add salt and pepper to taste. Cover and let stand for 30 minutes at room temperature to allow flavors to blend. Serve chilled or at room temperature.

THINK AHEAD
Make sambal up to 4 hours in advance. Cover and refrigerate. Stir before serving.

COOKS' NOTE
This recipe is also delicious when mango is used in place of the papaya.

SPICED CHICKPEA SAUCE

MAKES 2⅛ CUPS

1 - 14oz can chickpeas, drained and rinsed
2 garlic cloves, crushed
½ tsp ground cumin
¼ tsp tabasco
2 tbsp fresh lemon juice
5 tbsp tahini
5 tbsp water
½ cup sour cream
salt, black pepper

Place chickpeas, garlic, cumin, tabasco, lemon juice, tahini, water, and sour cream in a food processor or blender; pulse until smooth. Add salt and pepper to taste. Cover and refrigerate for 30 minutes to allow flavors to blend. Serve chilled.

THINK AHEAD
Make sauce up to 3 days in advance. Cover and refrigerate.

HONEY MISO SAUCE

MAKES ½ CUP

4 tbsp miso (see page 159)
4 tbsp honey
1 tbsp Dijon mustard
2 tbsp grated fresh ginger
2 garlic cloves, crushed
1½ tbsp soy sauce
1½ tbsp cider vinegar

Whisk miso, honey, mustard, ginger, garlic, soy sauce, and vinegar together until smooth. Cover and let stand for 30 minutes at room temperature to allow flavors to blend. Serve at room temperature.

THINK AHEAD
Make sauce up to 1 day in advance. Cover and store at room temperature.

CUCUMBER YOGURT RAITA

MAKES 2⅛ CUPS

1 unpeeled cucumber, seeded and grated
2 scallions, finely chopped
1 garlic clove, crushed
½ tbsp grated fresh ginger
2 tbsp finely chopped fresh mint leaves
3 tbsp fresh lemon juice
1⅔ cups Greek-style yogurt
salt, black pepper
1 tsp cumin seeds, toasted

Combine cucumber, scallions, garlic, ginger, mint, lemon juice, and yogurt or sour cream. Add salt and pepper to taste. Cover and refrigerate for 30 minutes to allow flavors to blend. Sprinkle with cumin seeds. Serve chilled.

THINK AHEAD
Make raita up to 1 day in advance. Cover and refrigerate. Stir before serving.

CILANTRO COCONUT SAUCE

MAKES 2⅛ CUPS

1 handful cilantro leaves
1 handful fresh mint leaves
4 garlic cloves, crushed
1 green chile, seeded and chopped
1 avocado, peeled, halved, and pitted
½ tsp ground cumin
1 tsp sugar
3 tbsp fresh lime juice
1½ cups coconut milk
salt, tabasco

Place cilantro, mint, garlic, chile, avocado, cumin, sugar, lime juice, and coconut milk in a food processor or blender; pulse to a purée. Add salt and tabasco to taste. Cover and refrigerate for 30 minutes to allow flavors to blend. Serve chilled.

THINK AHEAD
Make sauce up to 1 day in advance. Cover and refrigerate. Stir before serving.

COOKS' NOTE
To prevent discoloration, store in a bowl with plastic wrap, pressing directly on the sauce to prevent contact with air.

ROASTED PEPPER AND BASIL SALSA

MAKES 1 CUP

3 red peppers
2 garlic cloves, finely chopped
10 basil leaves, torn
1 tbsp red wine vinegar
3 tbsp olive oil
salt, black pepper

Grill, peel, and seed the peppers (see page 160). Cut into fine dice. Combine peppers, garlic, basil, vinegar, and oil. Add salt and pepper to taste. Cover and let stand for 30 minutes at room temperature to allow flavors to blend.

THINK AHEAD
Make salsa up to 1 day in advance but add basil not more than 2 hours before serving. Cover and refrigerate. Bring back to room temperature and stir before serving.

MAKING FLAVORED BUTTERS
Cut a piece of foil, approximately
10 x 8 inches. Spread the butter in
a block about 6 inches long and
2 inches thick in the middle of the foil.
Roll up.

Twist the ends tightly to form an even
shaped cylinder.

COOKS' NOTE
Flavored butters are practical and easy. They can
be made well in advance, frozen and sliced to
order. Place a cold slice of flavored butter on any
food hot off the grill to create a simple, flavorful
sauce with mininal effort.

CILANTRO CHILI BUTTER
MAKES 15 SERVINGS

16 tbsp unsalted butter, softened
1 handful cilantro leaves, chopped
1 fresh red chile, seeded and
  chopped

1 tbsp fresh lime juice
2 tsp salt
1 tsp black pepper

Place ingredients in a food processor or blender; pulse until well blended. Wrap in
foil (see left). Place in the freezer until hard, about 45 minutes. To serve, roll back
foil and cut into ½-inch slices. When slicing from frozen, warm the knife under
hot water first. After slicing, always tightly rewrap the unused
flavored butter roll in the foil before returning to refrigerator or freezer.

THINK AHEAD
Make up to 6 weeks in advance and refrigerate. Alternatively, make up to 9 months in advance and place in
freezer. To keep sliced butter chilled outdoors, float slices in a bowl of cold water and ice.

VARIATION
GARLIC PARSLEY BUTTER
MAKES 15 SERVINGS

Replace cilantro with the same amount of flat-leaf parsley. Replace lime juice with
the same amount of fresh lemon juice. Replace red chile with 5 crushed garlic cloves.

BLUE-CHEESE BUTTER
MAKES 15 SERVINGS

16 tbsp unsalted butter,
  softened

4oz (1 cup crumbled) blue cheese
2 tsp black pepper

Place ingredients in a food processor or blender; pulse until well blended. Wrap in
foil (see left). Place in the freezer until hard, about 45 minutes. To serve, roll back
foil and cut into ½-inch slices. When slicing from frozen, warm the knife under
hot water first. After slicing, always tightly rewrap the unused flavored butter roll in
the foil before returning to refrigerator or freezer.

THINK AHEAD
Make up to 6 weeks in advance and refrigerate. Alternatively, make up to 9 months in advance and place in
freezer. To keep sliced butter chilled outdoors, float slices in a bowl of cold water and ice.

VARIATION
BLACK OLIVE BUTTER
MAKES 15 SERVINGS

Replace blue cheese with ½ cup pitted black olives, such as kalamata or gaeta,
chopped. Add 3 tbsp thyme leaves and 1 tsp salt. Reduce black pepper by 1 tsp.

MAKING MAYONNAISE
Whisk the yolks until thick and creamy.

Add the oil in a steady stream.

MAYONNAISE

MAKES 1¼ CUPS
2 egg yolks
1 tsp Dijon mustard
1 tbsp red wine vinegar
½ tsp salt
pinch black pepper
⅔ cup canola oil
⅔ cup olive oil

Make sure that all the ingredients are at room temperature before you begin. Set a deep bowl on a cloth to prevent it from slipping as you whisk. Whisk the egg yolks, mustard, vinegar, salt, and pepper together in a bowl until thick and creamy, 1 minute (see left).
Combine the oils in a measuring cup. Whisk the oil into the egg yolk mixture a drop at a time until it thickens (see opposite). Add the remaining oil in a thin, steady stream, whisking constantly until thick and glossy. Whisk in any flavoring, if using, according to recipe variations opposite. Adjust seasoning, adding more mustard, vinegar, salt, or pepper to taste.

THINK AHEAD
Make mayonnaise up to 3 days in advance. Cover and refrigerate. Return to room temperature before stirring to prevent the mayonnaise from separating.

COOKS' NOTE
If the ingredients are too cold or the oil is added too quickly, the mayonnaise may separate. Don't throw it away! Combine 1 tsp vinegar and 1 tsp Dijon mustard in a clean bowl. Whisk in the separated mayonnaise drop by drop until the mixture reemulsifies.

USING STORE-BOUGHT MAYONNAISE

Use store-bought made mayonnaise when in need of a time saving shortcut or if health concerns are an issue for you. Seek out a good quality whole egg brand of mayonnaise and freshen the flavor by whisking in Dijon mustard, sugar, and red wine vinegar or lemon juice to taste.

USING A MACHINE

Follow recipe for mayonnaise. Place the egg yolks, mustard, vinegar, salt, pepper, and sugar with 3 tbsp of the oil in a food processor or blender; process until blended, 10 seconds. While the machine is running, pour in the remaining oil in a thin, steady stream, until the mixture emulsifies and becomes thick and glossy. Pulse in any flavoring, if using. Adjust seasoning, adding more mustard, vinegar, salt, or pepper to taste.

COOKS' NOTE
If using a food processor, depending on its capacity, you may need to stop the machine at intervals to scrape down the sides and over the base of the bowl with a spatula.

SAFETY WARNING ON RAW EGGS
Because of potential risk of salmonella, pregnant women, young children, and anyone with a weakened immune system should avoid eating raw eggs.
Make sure you use only the freshest (preferably organic) eggs, and if in doubt, substitute store-bought mayonnaise (see above).

ROASTED RED PEPPER AÏOLI

MAKES 1¼ CUPS
**2 red peppers
1 recipe mayonnaise (see page 142)**

Grill, peel, and seed the peppers (see page 160). Place in food processor or blender; pulse until smooth. Whisk pepper purée into the mayonnaise.

ROASTED GARLIC AÏOLI

MAKES 1¼ CUPS
**1 head of garlic
1 recipe mayonnaise (see page 142)
olive oil
salt and black pepper**

Slice off top of garlic, cutting through the cloves. Place cut-side up in oven tray. Drizzle with olive oil and sprinkle with salt and pepper. Preheat oven to 300°F. Roast garlic head until completely soft, 1 hour. Let cool. Squeeze out cloves from papery skins. Mash until smooth. Whisk into mayonnaise.

CHILI LIME MAYONNAISE

MAKES 1¼ CUPS
**1 fresh green chile, seeded and finely chopped
1 tbsp finely chopped cilantro leaves.
1 tbsp fresh lime juice
1 recipe mayonnaise (see page 142)**

Whisk chile, cilantro, and lime juice into mayonnaise.

SALADS & SIDES

SLOW-ROASTED TOMATO SALAD

SERVES 4

6 tomatoes, halved
2 garlic cloves, finely sliced
1 tsp honey
1 tbsp balsamic vinegar
1 tbsp olive oil
salt, black pepper
1 tbsp chopped flat-leaf parsley leaves
extra balsamic vinegar and
   olive oil to drizzle

Preheat oven to 300°F.
Place tomato halves cut side up in an oven tray. Place a garlic slice on top of each half. Drizzle with honey, vinegar, and oil. Sprinkle with salt and pepper. Roast until very soft and lightly charred, 1 hour. Sprinkle with parsley and drizzle with oil and vinegar. Serve chilled or at room temperature

THINK AHEAD
Roast tomatoes up to 1 day in advance. Cover and refrigerate.

PARSLEY, MINT, AND BULGUR SALAD WITH LEMON

SERVES 4

1½ cups bulgur wheat
1 cup boiling water
juice of 3 lemons
¼ cup olive oil
2 tsp salt
1 tsp black pepper
1 tsp ground sumac (optional, see cook's note)
4 medium tomatoes, seeded and diced
3 handfuls flat-leaf parsley leaves, roughly chopped
1 handful fresh mint leaves, torn

Place the bulgur wheat in a bowl. Cover with boiling water. Set aside until swollen and tender, 30 minutes. Drain well, pressing to squeeze out excess water. Return to the bowl. Pour in the lemon juice and oil. Add salt, pepper, and sumac (if using). Add tomatoes, parsley, and mint. Mix together until evenly combined. Serve chilled or at room temperature.

THINK AHEAD
Prepare ingredients as directed up to 1 day in advance, but do not mix. Cover and refrigerate. Mix up to 1 hour before serving.

COOKS' NOTE
Sumac is a dark burgundy colored seed with a distinctive citrus tang often used in Lebanese, Iranian, and Syrian cuisine. You can buy it in powdered form from Middle-Eastern stores or by mail order (see page 167). It gives this refreshing, lemony salad an extra kick, but is not essential.

CREAMY POTATO SALAD WITH CELERY AND CHIVES

SERVES 4

1½ lbs new potatoes, cut into
  bite-size pieces
1 tsp Dijon mustard
1 tbsp red wine vinegar
2 tbsp olive oil
1 tsp salt
½ tsp black pepper
4oz cream cheese
⅔ cup Greek-style yogurt or
  crème fraîche
2 celery stalks, finely diced
2½ tbsp finely chopped fresh chives
extra snipped fresh chives to garnish

Place potatoes in a large pan of cold water. Bring to the boil. Gently simmer until tender when pierced with the tip of a knife, but still firm, 10–15 minutes. Drain.

In large bowl, mix mustard, vinegar, oil, salt, and pepper until smooth. Add hot potatoes. Toss gently to coat each potato piece. Set aside for 30 minutes to allow flavors to combine.

Beat cream cheese and sour cream or crème fraîche until smooth. Stir in celery and chives. Mix gently with potatoes to coat evenly. Add salt and pepper to taste. Refrigerate for at least 1 hour before serving. Garnish with extra chives. Serve chilled or at room temperature.

THINK AHEAD
Make salad up to 1 day in advance. Cover and refrigerate.

COOKS' NOTE
If you can't find fresh chives, scallions are also excellent in this creamy, crunchy potato salad.

SESAME SOBA NOODLE SALAD

SERVES 4
2 tbsp sesame seeds
9oz soba noodles
3 tbsp shoyu (Japanese soy sauce)
1 tbsp sesame oil

Toast sesame seeds in a dry pan over a low heat until nutty and lightly colored, 5 minutes. Set aside. Cook noodles in a large pan of boiling water until tender but firm, 5 minutes. Drain and rinse in cold water to cool completely. Drain again. Place in a bowl. Add toasted seeds, shoyu, and oil. Mix gently to coat noodles. Serve chilled or at room temperature

THINK AHEAD
Prepare salad up to 6 hours in advance. Cover and refrigerate.

COOKS' NOTE
Soba noodles are made from buckwheat flour. These grayish brown Japanese noodles are available from Asian stores, healthfood shops, and most supermarkets. Alternatively, use Chinese egg noodles.

ASIAN NOODLE SALAD WITH CILANTRO AND LIME

SERVES 4

½ lb rice vermicelli noodles
1 medium carrot, diagonally sliced,
  then cut into fine strips
¼ cucumber, diagonally sliced,
  then cut into fine strips
4 scallions, diagonally sliced
2 fresh red chiles, seeded and
  finely sliced

2 tbsp chopped cilantro leaves
2 tbsp torn fresh mint leaves

FOR DRESSING
¼ cup fresh lime juice
¼ cup fish sauce
2 tsp sugar

Cook the noodles in a large pan of boiling water until tender but firm, 5 minutes. Drain, then rinse in cold water to cool completely. Drain again. Roughly snip noodles into smaller lengths with kitchen scissors.

For dressing, mix lime juice, fish sauce, and sugar until sugar dissolves. Gently toss noodles, carrot, cucumber, scallions, chile, cilantro, and mint with dressing until well mixed. Serve chilled or at room temperature.

THINK AHEAD
Prepare noodles, salad ingredients, and dressing up to 6 hours in advance. Store separately, covered and refrigerated. Combine ingredients up to 1 hour before serving. Cover and refrigerate.

SMOKY BLACK BEAN SALAD

SERVES 4

1⅓ cups dried black beans or
  2 - 14oz cans black beans,
  drained and rinsed

FOR DRESSING

2 garlic cloves, crushed
1 chipotle chile, seeded and finely
  chopped or 1 tsp chili powder
½ tsp ground cumin
½ tsp ground coriander
2 tsp salt
1 tsp black pepper
3 tbsp red wine vinegar
¼ cup olive oil
1 recipe salsa fresca (see page 133)
6 tbsp crumbled feta cheese, or
  queso fresco

If using dried beans, place in a large
pan with cold water to cover by 2 inches.
Bring to the boil. Boil hard for
10 minutes. Lower heat and simmer
until the beans are tender, 1–1½ hours.
If necessary, add hot water to keep
beans covered throughout the cooking
time. Drain thoroughly and set aside.

For dressing, combine garlic, chipotle
or chili powder, cumin, coriander, salt,
pepper, vinegar, and oil. If using dried
beans, pour dressing over hot cooked
beans. If using canned beans, place
dressing in a small pan, bring to the boil
and pour hot dressing over rinsed
canned beans. Mix gently to coat beans.
Add salt, pepper, and more chili powder
to taste. Set aside for 30 minutes to allow
flavors to combine.

Pour salsa fresca over beans. Sprinkle
with feta or queso fresco. Serve chilled
or at room temperature.

THINK AHEAD
Dress beans up to 1 day in advance. Cover and
refrigerate. Top with salsa and cheese up to 1 hour
before serving.

COOKS' NOTE
You can also use red kidney, black-eyed, or pinto
beans for this recipe.

SPICY PITA CHIPS

SERVES 4

4 pita breads
6 tbsp olive oil
4 garlic cloves
½ tsp crushed red pepper flakes
1 tsp dried oregano
1 tsp dried thyme
½ tsp salt
¼ tsp black pepper

Split pita breads open into two. Combine oil, garlic, red pepper flakes, oregano, thyme, salt, and pepper. Brush crumb sides of pita halves with spicy oil. Grill or bake according to instructions below. Remove to a wire rack and leave to cool. Break into large pieces and serve.

OUTDOOR
Grill over medium-hot coals until golden brown, 1–2 minutes per side.

INDOOR
Preheat oven to 350°F. Place oiled side up on baking sheet. Toast until golden brown, 5–8 minutes.

CRISPY GREEN LEAF SALAD

SERVES 4

1 iceberg lettuce heart, quartered
½ cup blue cheese, honey mustard or creamy chive dressing (see opposite)
salt, black pepper

Arrange the lettuce quarters on a platter and spoon over the dressing. Sprinkle with salt and pepper. Serve chilled or at room temperature.

COOKS' NOTE
Romaine lettuce hearts are also delicious with any of these dressings.

CREAMY CHIVE DRESSING

MAKES ½ CUP

1 tbsp finely chopped fresh chives
2 tsp Dijon mustard
1 tsp sugar
1 tbsp fresh lemon juice
2 tbsp olive oil
½ cup sour cream or crème fraîche
salt, black pepper

Mix together chives, mustard, sugar, lemon juice, oil, and sour cream or crème fraîche until thick and smooth. Add salt and pepper to taste.

THINK AHEAD
Make dressing up to 1 day in advance. Cover and refrigerate.

HONEY MUSTARD DRESSING

MAKES ½ CUP

1 garlic clove, crushed
1 tbsp honey
2 tbsp Dijon mustard
2 tbsp red wine vinegar
¼ cup olive oil
2 tbsp crème fraîche or sour cream
salt, black pepper

Mix together garlic, honey, mustard, vinegar, oil, and crème fraîche or sour cream until thick and smooth. Add salt and pepper to taste.

THINK AHEAD
Make dressing up to 1 day in advance. Cover and refrigerate.

BLUE-CHEESE DRESSING

MAKES ½ CUP

4 tbsp blue cheese, crumbled
1 tbsp finely chopped scallions
2 tbsp red wine vinegar
2 tbsp sour cream
¼ cup olive oil
salt, black pepper

Mix together blue cheese, scallions, vinegar, sour cream, and oil until combined. Add salt and pepper to taste.

THINK AHEAD
Make dressing up to 1 day in advance. Cover and refrigerate.

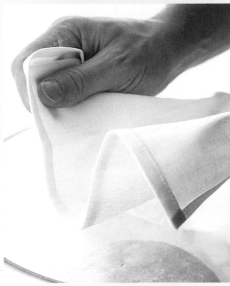

MAKING FOCACCIA DOUGH
Knead the dough until it is smooth, light, and elastic.

Cover the dough with a cloth and let rise until doubled in size.

FOCACCIA

SERVES 4–6

3½ cups all-purpose flour
2 tsp salt
1⅓ cups lukewarm water
2 tsp active dried yeast

2 tbsp olive oil
2 tsp fresh rosemary leaves
salt and pepper to sprinkle

Place the flour in a bowl. Make a well in the middle and sprinkle the salt around the edges. Pour the water into the well and sprinkle with the yeast. Let stand 5 minutes to allow the yeast to soften, then stir to dissolve. Add olive oil to the mixture.

Draw in the rest of the flour to make a rough, sticky dough. Turn out onto a lightly floured surface and knead for 10 minutes, until smooth, light, and elastic (see top left). Put back into the bowl, cover with a cloth, and leave until doubled in size, about 1½ hours (see bottom left).

Preheat the oven to 400°F. Deflate the dough by pressing down with the palm of your hand. Roll out into a flat round about 9 inches across and place on an oiled baking sheet. Sprinkle with rosemary leaves, salt, and pepper, or top according to the variations below. Cover with a cloth and leave until risen, about 30 minutes. Bake until bread is puffed and crisp on top, about 30 minutes. Cool on a wire rack. Serve warm, sprinkled with coarse salt and cut into wedges.

THINK AHEAD
Make and knead the dough and leave to rise in the refrigerator for 8–12 hours. Let stand at room temperature for half an hour before punching down and shaping again. Rise again and bake according to the recipe. Alternatively, bake focaccia 1 day in advance and reheat in a hot oven for 15 minutes.

POTATO FOCACCIA WITH THYME

SERVES 4–6

1 recipe unbaked
  focaccia dough (see above)

FOR TOPPING
1lb baby potatoes
1½ cups grated Gruyère cheese
2 tsp fresh thyme leaves
¼ cup crème fraîche, optional

Prepare dough according to recipe above. Leave to rise through the second step. Preheat oven to 400°F. Cut potatoes into ¼-inch slices. Bring a pan of salted water to a boil, add the potatoes, bring back to a boil and cook until the centers are just tender when pricked, about 5 minutes. Drain well and cool.

Shape dough according to the third step in the recipe above. Sprinkle half the cheese on top of the shaped dough. Arrange the potato slices over cheese. Top with remaining cheese. Sprinkle with thyme, salt, and pepper. Dot potatoes with crème fraîche. Bake until bread is puffed and topping is crisp, about 30 minutes.

ROASTED ONION FOCACCIA WITH ROSEMARY

SERVES 4–6

1 recipe unbaked focaccia dough
  (see above)

FOR TOPPING
3 red onions, cut into wedges
1 tbsp olive oil
1½ cups grated Gruyère cheese
2 tsp chopped fresh rosemary leaves
salt, black pepper

Prepare dough according to recipe above. Leave to rise through the second step. Preheat the oven to 400°F. Place onions in an oven tray. Drizzle with oil. Roast until soft and wilted, 30 minutes. Cool.

Shape dough according to the third step in the recipe above. Sprinkle half the cheese evenly on top of the shaped dough. Arrange onions over cheese. Top with remaining cheese. Sprinkle with rosemary, salt, and pepper. Bake until bread is puffed and topping is crisp, about 30 minutes.

THE MENUS

NUEVO TEX MEX
A real crowd-pleaser: south of the border classics meet fresher, bolder flavors for great, gutsy food. Everyone will love this fun fiesta of wraps, chips, salsas, and dips. Icy cold beers, please!

Creamy Avocado Salsa
(see page 132)
Store-bought tortilla chips

•

Spicy Lime Chicken Wings
(see page 101)
Chargrilled Quesadillas with
Spicy Cilantro
(see page 128)

•

Spiced Beef Fajitas with Salsa
Fresca and Guacamole
(see page 38)
Smoky Black Bean Salad
(see page 151)

•

Premium brand chocolate ice cream

TASTE OF MOROCCO
Aromatic spices, fragrant herbs and refreshing citrus flavors make this North African-inspired menu a delight for all the senses.

Honey Harissa Kofte
(see page 60)
Spiced Chickpea Sauce
(see page 137)
Spicy Pita Chips
(see page 152)

•

Coriander Lamb Pita Wraps
(see page 58)
Parsley, Mint, and Bulgur Salad
with Lemon
(see page 147)

•

Grill Roasted Sweet
Spiced Oranges
(see page 126)

VEGETARIAN GRILL
As the vegetables come hot off the grill, arrange them on large platters, spoon over the sauces, and let everyone help themselves. You can make the focaccia and sauces a day ahead; refer to our THINK AHEAD *notes.*

Creamy Blue-Cheese Sauce
(see page 133)
Spicy Pita Chips
(see page 152)

•

Chargrilled Eggplant Slices
with Lemon Tahini Sauce
(see page 122)
Chargilled Zucchini with
Roasted Pepper and Basil Salsa
(see page 123)
Chargrilled New Potato Skewers
(see page 120)
Roast Onion Focaccia with
Rosemary
(see page 155)

BARBECUE ON THE BEACH
A beach is, of course, not essential. The backyard will do, but plenty of lemon wedges and paper napkins are a must. We suggest a well-chilled crisp white wine to accompany this celebration of seafood.

Clams in Cilantro Chili Butter
(see page 74)
Squid with Tomato Avocado Salsa
(see page 69)

•

Provençal Seafood Grillade with
Lemon Fennel Dressing and Roast
Garlic Aïoli
(see page 86)
A crusty baguette

•

Bowlful of summer berries

REAL FAST MENU FOR ENTERTAINING
High-flavor, low-input dishes for the time-challenged cook. You can make this menu a last-minute affair or use our THINK AHEAD *notes if you prefer to plan in advance.*

Honey Soy Chicken Wings
(see page 101)
Spicy Peanut Sauce
(see page 136)

•

Rosemary Peppered Pork Chops
(see page 44)
Chargrilled Tomatoes
(see page 120)
Crispy Green Leaf Salad with
Creamy Chive Dressing
(see page 152)

•

Chargrilled Nectarines
(see page 125)
Premium brand vanilla ice cream

ISLAND BARBECUE

A totally tropical menu. Warm spices, hot chili, savory seasonings, and a dash of dark rum will bring the sunny flavors of the Caribbean to your backyard.

Lemon Chili Shrimp
(see page 66)
Pineapple Lime Salsa
(see page 134)
•
Skewered Bajaan Chicken
(see page 96)
Chargrilled Squash with Jerked Honey Rum Glaze
(see page 123)
Chargilled Corn on the Cob with Cilantro Chili butter
(see page 119)
•
Grill Roasted Cinnamon Rum Bananas
(see page 126)
Premium brand vanilla ice cream

ASIAN FUSION

Eastern traditions meet western trends in this simple, fresh and stylish menu bursting with vibrant flavors.

Spicy Masala Shrimp
(see page 64)
Thai Spiced Chicken Wings
(see page 100)
Cilantro Coconut Sauce
(see page 138)
•
Spiced Soy Duck
(see page 113)
Sesame Soba Noodle Salad
(see page 148)
Fresh Papaya Sambal
(see page 137)
•
Platter of chilled fresh tropical fruit

TUSCAN GRILL

A great menu if cooking for a crowd. You can bake the focaccia, prepare the lamb, and grill the bruschetta and peppers a day ahead. A rich and rustic red wine perfectly complements this sensational sun-drenched menu.

Char-Roasted Lemon Oregano Peppers on Bruschetta
(see page 129)
•
Lamb with Anchovy, Prosciutto, and Parsley **(see page 54)**
Slow Roast Tomato Salad
(see page 147)
Potato Focaccia with Thyme
(see page 155)
•
Grill Roasted Honey Orange Figs
(see page 126)

NOUVELLE GRILL

A thoroughly modern menu that combines global influences with contemporary inspirations.

Radish Tzatziki
(see page 135)
Spicy Pita Chips
(see page 152)
•
Shrimp with Tamarind Recado
(see page 67)
Pineapple Lime Salsa
(see page 134)
•
Spice-crusted Tuna with Thai Citrus Dressing
(see page 78)
Asian Noodle Salad with Cilantro and Lime
(see page 150)
•
Grill-Roasted Lemon Liqueur Strawberries
(see page 126)

NEW AMERICAN GRILL

A new look at the traditional cookout. All the family favorites—drums, ribs, and steaks, with the influence of Asian and Latin flavors to replace the standard barbecue sauce. Our potato salad is as creamy as Mom's, but we make it lighter to suit today's tastes.

Honey Mustard Chicken Drumsticks
(see page 102)
Spiced Hoisin Ribs
(see page 48)
•
Chargrilled T-bone Steak with Chimi Churri Sauce
(see page 34)
Chargrilled Tomatoes
(see page 120)
Creamy Potato Salad with Celery and Chives
(see page 148)
•
Premium brand vanilla ice cream

NOTES FROM THE COOKS ON INGREDIENTS

ACHIOTE SEASONING is a Mexican blend of ground annatto seeds (see below), oregano, cumin, cinnamon, pepper, and cloves. It is available powdered or as a paste from mail-order or specialty stores (see page 167), or you can make your own (see page 23).

ANNATTO, also called achiote (see page 23), are the rusty red seeds of the annatto tree. Annatto is known as the saffron of Latin America, where it is used for its brick red color and earthy flavor.

CAPERS are the pickled bud of the caper plant. Always drain well before using.

CARAWAY SEEDS are aromatic seeds with a nutty, mildly anise flavor, widely used in Central European baking and cooking.

CARDAMOM is best used freshly ground since its fragrance diminishes with time. Crush lightly, open, discard the pods and grind the seeds (see page 161). If you are buying cardamom in the pod, choose green not brown cardamom for the recipes in this book.

CHILES (see page 18) come fresh, as powder, or as flakes. There are over 200 different varieties of fresh chiles, varying in color, size, shape, and heat. When buying fresh chiles, make sure the stem is still on and that it is as fresh as possible; avoid any that have no stem. As a general rule, the smaller the chile the hotter it is. Capsaicin, the substance in chiles responsible for their heat, can cause a very painful burning sensation if it comes into contact with the eyes or areas of sensitive skin. Make sure you wash your hands thoroughly after handling chiles. To reduce the level of heat, remove the seeds before using (see page 160).
Scotch bonnets are fresh, lantern-shaped chiles from the Caribbean

with a fruity, citrus flavor and fiery heat. If you cannot find them fresh, use Carribbean hot pepper sauce as an alternative and add drop by drop to taste.
Chili powder is a hot seasoning of ground dried chiles, garlic, oregano, cumin, and coriander. Pure chili powders are ground from one variety of chile without the additon of other spices and flavorings.
Ancho chili powder is made from ground dried poblano chiles from the Americas. It is deep reddish brown in color with a mildly pungent, rich, sun-dried flavor.
Kashmiri chili powder is made from powdered Kashmiri chiles from India; it has a sweetish, pungent flavor without a burning heat.
Chipotles in adobo are dried smoked jalapeño chiles, pickled and canned in a piquant sauce made from chiles, herbs, and vinegar. They are available by mail order or from specialty stores (see page 167).

CHILI SAUCE is available in many different varieties. We use two types, and both can be found in large supermarkets or in Asian stores.
Chinese hot chili sauce (see page 18) is made from chiles, salt and vinegar; if unavailable, use standard hot chili sauce as an alternative.
Thai sweet chili sauce (see page 19), flavored with ginger and garlic as well as sugar, salt, vinegar, and chiles, is often labeled "dipping sauce for chicken." If you can't find it, make your own. Combine ⅔ cup rice or cider vinegar with ¼ cup sugar in a small pan; stir to dissolve. Bring to a boil and simmer until syrupy, 5 minutes. Stir in ¼ tsp salt, 1 finely chopped garlic clove, ½ tsp grated ginger, and 1 seeded and finely chopped red chile. Cool before using. Cover and refrigerate for up to 1 week.

CHIPOTLES IN ADOBO (see chiles)

COCONUT MILK is available in cans from Asian stores and large supermarkets. Shake well before opening.

FISH SAUCE (see page 19) is thin, salty, brown sauce made from fermented fish and used extensively in Southeast Asian cooking. It is available from large supermarkets, Asian stores, or mail order (see page 167). We use Thai fish sauce called nam pla; use soy sauce as an alternative.

FIVE-SPICE POWDER is a Chinese spice blend of ground cloves, cinnamon, fennel, star anise, and Szechuan pepper.

GINGER in its fresh form has a very different flavor from ground. Do not substitute ground ginger for fresh. Wrap and store fresh ginger in the refrigerator for up to 3 weeks. Cut off the skin with a sharp knife before grating (see page 160).
Pickle ginger (see page 20) is the Japanese condiment for sushi. It is easily recognized by its pink color and is available in jars.

GREEK-STYLE YOGURT is made from cow's or sheep's milk and is rich, creamy, and flavorful. Use half sour cream and half plain yogurt as an alternative.

HOISIN SAUCE (see page 20) is a slightly sweet, thick, dark brown sauce made from soy beans, garlic, and spices. It will keep indefinitely in a covered jar.

LEMON GRASS (see page 21) comes in long stalks and has a fragrant citrus flavor and aroma. Use only the tender inner stem as the the outer leaves are tough. Lemon grass freezes very well, so you can buy it in quantity, freeze and use it as needed. As an alternative, use ½ tsp each of grated lime and lemon zest for 1 lemon grass stalk.

MIRIN is Japanese rice wine. It is sweeter than sake and used only for cooking. Use medium dry sherry as an alternative.

MISO (see page 20) is Japanese fermented soy bean paste. It is salty but highly nutritious. It is available in Asian stores, health food stores, and large supermarkets. It comes in various colors and keeps indefinitely in the refrigerator.

MUSTARD comes in many forms, but we prefer to use smooth French Dijon. For a coarser texture, use grainy Dijon mustard.

PANCETTA is flavorful Italian bacon. Store wrapped in the refrigerator for up to 3 weeks. Use bacon as an alternative.

PEPPER should be freshly ground or cracked for maximum flavor. A good pepper grinder is an essential item for any cook who values flavor.

POMEGRANATE MOLASSES (see page 20)—also referred to as syrup or concentrate—is made by boiling down pomegranate juice to a thick, dark brown liquid with a distinctive sweet-sour flavor. It's a favorite flavoring across the Middle East, but especially in Iran, Syria, and Lebanon. It is available in bottles from Middle-Eastern stores or by gourmet mail order (see page 167). Date molasses, which is readily found in healthfood stores, can be used as an alternative.

PRESERVED LEMONS are whole lemons pickled in salty lemon juice and used as a flavoring and condiment in Moroccan cooking.

PROSCIUTTO is Italian raw ham that has been seasoned, salt-cured, and air-dried.

QUESO FRESCO is a fresh cow's milk cheese with a tangy flavor. It has a dry and crumbly texture and distinctive bright, white color. Look for it in Mexican groceries. Alternatively, use feta cheese.

RICE NOODLES are Asian noodles made from rice flour. Use Chinese dried egg noodles as an alternative. Cook according to the package instructions.

SAKE is Japan's famous rice wine, widely used as a flavoring in Japanese sauces and marinades. Use dry sherry as an alternative.

SALT should always be sea salt, whether coarse or fine. The quality of salt matters. Different salts have different flavors and different degrees of saltiness. Salt draws out the moisture in meat, so we always season with it only after grilling.

SCOTCH BONNETS (see chiles)

SESAME OIL (see page 20) is best when it is one of the Asian brands, and is extracted from toasted sesame seeds. Don't confuse this with the lighter sesame oil with a less intense flavor that is sold in healthfood stores.

SOBA NOODLES are very fine Japanese buckwheat noodles, available in Asian stores, healthfood stores, and large supermarkets. Use Chinese dried egg noodles as an alternative. Cook according to the package instructions.

SOY SAUCE is a major seasoning in Asian cooking. It is available in a number of varieties, ranging in color and flavor. We use light soy sauce when we wish to preserve the color of the food but dark soy sauce has a richer flavor. **Japanese soy sauce,** called **shoyu,** is sweeter, lighter and less salty; use light soy sauce as an alternative.

SPICES should be bought whole and toasted and ground yourself, for the best flavor (see page 161). Even if you store them for a month or so, your home-ground spices will still be more flavorful than anything you buy already ground from the supermarket.

TAHINI is a paste made from grinding roasted sesame seeds. It is sold in jars in large supermarkets, and healthfood and Middle-Eastern stores. Shake well before using.

TAMARIND (see page 20) has a bright, sharp, tangy flavor. It is used mostly in Southeast Asian and Middle-Eastern cooking. It is available as jars of paste or concentrate or in blocks of sticky pulp. To use the pulp, dissolve in boiling water and strain out the seeds: use ½ cup pulp to 1 cup water for a thick paste. It will keep in the refrigerator for up to 3 days, or you can freeze it in ice cube trays. Tamarind pulp and paste are available from Asian, Middle-Eastern, and Hispanic stores, or by gourmet mail order (see page 167). Use freshly squeezed lime juice as an alternative.

VINEGAR comes in a variety of forms. **Red wine vinegar** (see page 21) and **white wine vinegar** have different flavors and levels of acidity and should not be used interchangeably. **Balsamic vinegar** (see page 21) is a widely available Italian vinegar; it is dark in color with a sweet, pungent flavor. **Cider vinegar** is a mellow, fruity vinegar made from apple cider. **Rice vinegar** (see page 21) with its subtly sweet, mellow flavor, is used extensively in Japanese cooking. It is available in Asian stores and healthfood stores. Cider vinegar can be used as an alternative.

WASABI is a pungent green horseradish used in Japanese cuisine. It is available in dried powder form in cans and as a paste in tubes (see page 20). Use horseradish sauce as an alternative.

WHITE TRUFFLE OIL has a rich, earthy flavor and aroma and is delicious drizzled on pasta, risotto, vegetables, and salads. It is available in small bottles from specialty or Italian stores, or from gourmet mail order (see page 167).

ESSENTIAL SKILLS

GRILLING AND PEELING PEPPERS

Grill peppers over a hot outdoor flame or under a preheated broiler. Turn as needed until blackened on all sides, 10–15 minutes. Place in a plastic bag or a bowl with a plate on top and allow them to cool. Peel off the skin using the tip of a small knife. Cut the peppers into quarters and remove the core. Scrape away seeds and discard.

REMOVING SEEDS FROM A CHILE

Halve the chiles lengthwise with a small, sharp knife. Scape out the seeds and cut away the white ribs from each half. Wash hands after handling chiles.

CHOPPING AN ONION

Peel the onion, leaving the root end on. Cut the onion in half and lay one half, cut side down, on a chopping board. With a sharp knife cut horizontally toward the root end, and then vertically. Be sure to cut just to the root but not through it. Finally, cut the onion crosswise into diced pieces.

PEELING A GARLIC CLOVE

Set the flat side of the knife on top and strike it with your fist. This action will loosen the skin, allowing it to peel away easily by using your fingers. Discard the skin.

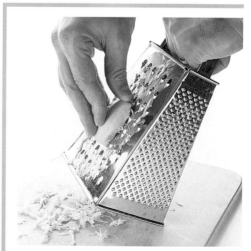

GRATING FRESH GINGER

Use a sharp knife or vegetable peeler to cut away the skin from the ginger. Grate the ginger, making sure to grate with the grain and not against it.

GRINDING WHOLE SPICES

Whole spices may be ground or cracked by hand in a mortar. Alternatively, to coarse grind or crack spices, place them in a resealable plastic bag and crush them with rolling pin or heavy saucepan. For large quantities, use a blender or food processor.

TOASTING SPICES

Place a dry cast-iron pan over a medium-hot heat until hot, 2 minutes. Add spices and toast, shaking the pan, until the spices are dark and aromatic, 5 minutes. Remove from pan and cool.

PEELING AND CHOPPING CITRUS

Cut a slice from the top and the bottom of the fruit. Cut away the rind, pith, and skin, working from top to bottom and following the curve of the fruit. Slice the peeled fruit crosswise into ¼-inch slices. Stack and chop the slices finely.

SEEDING TOMATOES

Cut the tomato in half crosswise. Gently squeeze each tomato half, pushing out the seeds with your fingertips.

MAKING CITRUS WEDGES

Cut the fruit in half lengthwise. Place cut side down on a board. Trim the stalk ends and discard. Cut each half across into 4 wedges.

INDEX

AUTHORS' ACKNOWLEDGMENTS

We would like to thank:
Our three very special teams, who are, if you like, the rocks on
which this enterprise is built.
The Books for Cooks team, but especially Victoria Blashford
Snell, Jennifer Joyce, Kimiko Barber, and Ursula Ferrigno.
Their passion for food, both contemporary and traditional,
remains a constant inspiration and we are eternally grateful for
their willingness to share their discoveries with us.
The Covent Garden team, Stuart Jackman, Julia Pemberton
Hellums, and Sally Somers for being just so fast, just so flexible,
just so ready to do it!
But perhaps this book really belongs to the studio team and
especially Ian O'Leary, for being ready, willing and able to get
out of the studio into the big outdoors. Things began pleasantly
enough down on the farm in the late summer sunshine, but we
had to work our way through a four seasons' worth of weather to
arrive at that bitterly cold day in December in our back garden.
Photography in torrential rain was never so much fun.

MAIL ORDER SOURCES

ADRIANA'S CARAVAN
409 Vanderbilt Street
Brooklyn, NY 11218
800-316-0820
www.adrianascaravan.com
*Catalog available. Herbs, spices,
condiments, and ethnic ingredients from
around the world, including tamarind
concentrate, pomegranate molasses, and
Thai sweet chili sauce.*

DEAN & DELUCA
560 Broadway
New York, NY 10012
800-221-7714
www.dean-deluca.com
*Catalog available. Luxury ingredients
and specialty foods from around the
world, including Thai sweet chili sauce,
white truffle oil, pomegranite molasses,
and tamarind concentrate.*

KATAGIRI
224 East 59th Street
New York, NY 10016
212-683-4419
www.katagiri.com
Japanese specialty ingredients.

MO-HOTTA-MO-BETTA
PO Box 4136
San Luis Obispo, CA 93403
800-462-3220
www.mohotta.com
*Catalog available. Powdered chiles and
other Southwestern ingredients.*

MING'S PANTRY
www.mingspantry.com
*Online provider of Chinese and Asian
food products, including hot chile sauces
and rice vinegar.*

PENZEYS SPICES
PO Box 933
Muskego, WI 53150
414-679-7207
www.penzeys.com
*Catalog available. Herbs, spices, and
seasonings.*

SUR LA TABLE
Catalog Division
1765 Sixth Avenue South
Seattle, Washington
800-243-0852
www.surlatable.com
*Catalog available. Tools for the cook,
including heavy-duty tongs, hinged grill
racks, ridged cast-iron grill pans, and
instant-read thermometers.*

PENDERY'S
www.penderys.com
*Online provider of chiles and spices and
other Latin American food products.*

CHEF'S
PO Box 620048
Dallas, TX 75262
800-338-3232
www.chefscatalog.com
*Catalog available. Professional
restaurant equipment for the home
chef, including heavy-duty tongs, hinged
grill racks, ridged grill pans and
instant-read thermometers.*

HOW WE MAKE OUR BOOKS

In 1983, a tiny bookstore with a unique concept opened in London's Notting Hill. BOOKS FOR COOKS is a book store run by cooks for cooks, selling only cookbooks, teaching cooking classes, cooking from the books, and serving up the results in a tiny restaurant among the bookshelves.

I work in the store, cook in the kitchen, and teach in the school. It's true that I acquired my technical training as a professional chef, but, to my mind, my real culinary education began the day I crossed the threshold of BOOKS FOR COOKS. It's from my students and customers that I learn most about the way people live, cook, and eat today, and it's this experience that informs the way we make our books. Real food for real life is our motto, and each title is specially devised to meet the needs of today's busy cooks.

I'm lucky enough to work in a team of dedicated food lovers. We research, test, photograph, write, design, and edit our books from start to finish. All the ingredients are bought at ordinary shops and tested in a domestic kitchen. Our recipes are designed to be cooked at home. Oh yes, and it's all real food in the photographs!

You can write, phone, fax, or e-mail us any time.

We'd love to hear from you.

BOOKS FOR COOKS
4 BLENHEIM CRESCENT
LONDON W11 1NN
TEL. 020-07221-1992
FAX. 020-07221-1517

info@booksforcooks.com